SPI
EGE
L&G
RAU

ALSO BY ADAM LANGER

Ellington Boulevard

The Washington Story

Crossing California

My Father's Bonus March

My Father's Bonus March

ADAM LANGER

SPIEGEL & GRAU

New York

2009

Published in the United States by Spiegel & Grau, an imprint of The Random House Publishing Group, a division of Random House, Inc., New York.

SPIEGEL & GRAU and Design is a trademark of Random House, Inc.

Grateful acknowledgment is made to the following for permission to quote from copyrighted material:

The February 12, 1982, letter sent from Barbara Tuchman to Dr. Seymour S. Langer is reprinted with the permission of Lucy T. Eisenberg, Tuchman's literary executor.

Excerpts of lyrics written by Al Carmines for his musical *The Bonus Army* are used with the permission of executor Edward G. Carmines.

A portion of Lou Henry Hoover's undated 1932 letter to her son Allan Hoover is used with the permission of Timothy Walch, director of the Herbert Hoover Presidential Library.

Portions of correspondence between the author and the National Personnel Records Center are reprinted here with the permission of the National Personnel Records Center.

Library of Congress Cataloging-in-Publication Data
Langer, Adam.
    My father's bonus march / Adam Langer.
        p.   cm.
    ISBN 978-0-385-52372-1 (alk. paper)
    1. Langer, Adam—Childhood and youth. 2. Fathers and sons—United States—
Biography. 3. Langer, Seymour, 1925–2005. 4. Langer, Adam—Family. 5. Bonus
Expeditionary Forces. I. Title.
    HQ755.85.L345 2009
    306.874'2092—dc22
    [B]   2009012842

Printed in the United States of America on acid-free paper

www.spiegelandgrau.com

9 8 7 6 5 4 3 2 1

First Edition

Book design by Caroline Cunningham

To Nora

and in memory of:

Seymour Sidney Langer (1925–2005)

and Studs Terkel (1912–2008)

But when he comes to die, he's got something on his mind called "Rosebud." What does that mean?

—Herman J. Mankiewicz and Orson Welles, *Citizen Kane*

Prologue

Stories I Know

People are so soon gone; let us catch them.

VIRGINIA WOOLF, *The Waves*

2007

My daughter is two years old, and she and I are sitting on the front steps outside my mother's house on Mozart Street in West Rogers Park on the North Side of Chicago. The sun has long since set and it's way past Nora's bedtime, but she shows no sign of falling asleep anytime soon, so I've been telling her stories about the neighborhood.

This is the same stoop where I would sit with my dad when he was still alive, I say, the same place where the two of us would watch and greet the neighbors going by—Loping Leemie on his way to the Jewish academy; Mr. Primack with his briefcase, off to work; Rabbi Michael Small, cigar in hand, heading for his shul on California and Albion.

A peaceful neighborhood, I tell Nora, a good place to grow up. In the 1970s, we never locked our doors. When we went out, we wouldn't even take our house keys along—until the night we returned to find our side door open, the dresser drawers upturned, clothes and papers everywhere. Our lockbox was gone, the one full of silver dollars my mom had received from her mother.

I ask Nora if I should tell her more about this block.

She nods, so I keep going.

Well, I say, see that house across the street, the one that's a little farther back than the others? An old couple lived there with their motorcycle-riding son, who moved out when I was a kid. When the blizzard of 1979 hit Chicago and the city didn't plow our streets, everybody on our block except the couple across the street pitched in twenty dollars to hire a private tow-truck driver to shovel. Everything got shoveled except their parking space. Their car just stood there like an igloo on asphalt until the woman sheepishly ran out with her twenty-dollar bill, and then everyone started working together to dig out her car.

As the night grows darker, I tell Nora more little stories about our old neighbors—Mrs. Golnick, who rushed over to our house the moment after she learned hers had been robbed; Sol Zimmerman, who dispatched a dead mouse from our kitchen when my mother and I were too frightened to do it ourselves; Irv Ellis, the onetime high school basketball star; Mr. Joe Small, the one-man neighborhood watch committee; Dr. Friedman, whose sister taught me in Hebrew school; an Orthodox Jewish man who wore shiny black shoes and played catch with me—he told me he used to play for the Brooklyn Dodgers.

I tell Nora more stories about myself, too. This is the same block where I'd ride up and down on my red tricycle with its Mickey Mouse bell and later on my yellow Schwinn, I tell her, the same block where I'd walk to kindergarten with my pal Beth Goldberg and debate the existence of God. "He's everywhere!" she'd say. "But how can He be everywhere?" I'd demand.

I say that these are the same steps where I'd play ball-against-the-wall after school with a white rubber ball and a Ron Santo mitt. "Play ball, Adam," Joe Small would shout whenever he saw me, and when I was done, he'd tell me about the trips he'd taken to Vegas, the appraised Omega watch he'd purchased there with his winnings, the Phyllis Diller show he'd seen. On weekends, my grade school pals and I would play Wiffle ball, making up our own rules—hit my dad's black Ford, get a ground-rule double; smack the ball over Mr. Small's red Lincoln, get a home run.

But I don't know how much Nora understands of what I'm telling her. It's really late, I finally say; it's time to go to bed. See, everybody's lights are off; everyone is asleep. The Friedmans are asleep and the Smalls are asleep and the Seruyas are asleep and the dogs and the cats and the squirrels and the birds are asleep, so maybe we should go to sleep, too.

But Nora says no.

"Okay," I say. "What do you want to do?"

"More stories, Papa," Nora says. "Tell more stories."

And at this moment, I realize that this stoop where my daughter and I are sitting, this street, this neighborhood in this city, this is the place that first made me want to become a writer, listening to our neighbors' stories, looking at houses and imagining what was going on inside. And at this moment, I realize, too, that this is what I still miss most about my father—the stories he isn't here to tell me anymore, the stories he never got around to telling me at all. I long to hear the stories about where he grew up, a place he never took me, the stories about his dreams, which he never shared.

"All right," I say to Nora, "let's tell more stories."

CHICAGO
(2006)

I

Memories of my father, a brilliant but contradictory man who was so present in my life and yet sometimes so distant and difficult to know, begin to return to me, appropriately enough, when I'm flying twenty thousand feet above the ground, looking down at the city where he and I were both born. It's wintertime, and I'm sitting in the window seat of a half-empty Embraer RJ-145, flying from Indianapolis to

Chicago, where I will board another plane to head to New York. My dad died two months ago, in November, at the age of eighty, and this will be the first time I will ever pass through Chicago without stopping at my parents' house.

The last plane ride I ever took with both my mom and dad was in 1978, when I was ten; we went to San Francisco for Memorial Day weekend. At the time, little seemed remarkable about our trip—we stayed at the Stanford Court Hotel, dined at Kan's in Chinatown, watched the D'Oyly Carte Opera Company perform *H.M.S. Pinafore,* hung out with one of my dad's old medical school pals, a chatterbox named Stan, who had struck it rich in Australian opal mines and referred to himself in the third person. I wore a brown nubbly suit to meet Stan; he told me I looked like David Copperfield.

But after we returned to Chicago, for more than the next twenty-five years, my father never left the state of Illinois. Sometimes, he'd talk about taking a trip to Williamsburg, Virginia, to view Civil War sites; about driving to Poughkeepsie, New York, to visit me in college, and to West Branch, Iowa, to research a book he'd always wanted to write about the 1932 Bonus March, a historical incident that fascinated him. He talked about taking a plane to London and leaving America for the first time; and one time not all that long ago about flying to Minnesota so that he could find a doctor at the Mayo Clinic who might be able to help him.

But he never went any of those places.

My dad, who rarely seemed to bother with introspection, never talked much about himself to me. He didn't talk about his inner life, never told me how he felt about flying or why he eventually stopped, but he never seemed to like giving control to anyone else—he boasted about once being on a plane that was taking too long to leave its gate; he insisted the flight attendants open the exit door so that he and my mother could get out, grab their luggage, and go back home.

That was the man I knew—doing everything his way, always in a rush. If it couldn't be done fast, it wasn't worth doing. He told me that on a trip to Los Angeles before I was born, he and my mom were in the audience of a sitcom and he had had enough of the show.

"You can't leave, sir," the usher said.

"Like hell I can't," my dad replied.

Yep, that was the dad I knew.

When I close my eyes, I can still easily picture my father. He was a broad-shouldered man, stocky, crew-cutted, and he stood five seven, just about the same height as I am. He wore black or brown dress shoes and Brooks Brothers button-down shirts—white or light blue, pale yellow in the 1970s. He walked with a limp and during the last years of his life, he had considerable difficulty with his knees and hips; still, he always moved fast, as if he was on his way to someplace more important, and if he was ever feeling any pain, save for the occasional moan of *"Oy vey,"* he wouldn't let you know about it. His default facial expression split the difference between knowing smirk and dubious sneer, as if he was in on a joke he wouldn't bother telling you, or as if you'd just told him something but he wasn't certain he believed you. "I don't know if I do or I don't," he liked to say. "I don't know if it's true or it isn't." Tough guy to get to know, even if you saw him every day.

Earlier tonight, when this plane took off from Indianapolis, a light snow was falling, but the night is now clear and the plane is flying relatively low; this is a short flight, only about a half hour in the air, and as we begin our approach to O'Hare Airport, I look out my window at the lights of Chicago. My father worked for more than fifty years as a radiologist, and looking at the city below me, I can almost envision an entire X-ray of his life developing—just about every place he ever went is becoming visible through this small window. I can actually make out where he was born, where he grew up, where he lived, where he worked, and where he died. And in everything I can see tonight, in all the lights and in all the blackness, are fragments of stories he told—in my mind, those stories are all the pieces I still have of him.

From this window, I can see Chicago's old West Side, which was essentially the Jewish ghetto when my dad was born there on March 16, 1925, in Chicago's Lying-In Hospital, the son of immigrants Rebecca and Samuel Langer. My dad was born with the name Sidney Langer, but he was hospitalized for pneumonia at the age of two and his parents changed his first name to Seymour, on the advice of a rabbi, to fool the dybbuk so that the boy would survive.

My dad's father was a hardworking army veteran who served as a mule skinner during World War I, when mules were still used for pulling heavy artillery. I know little about my father's European ancestors—the only story I remember my dad telling me about them concerned a cousin who supposedly served in the Polish army and fought the Russians during World War I. As for my grandfather, my father said he came over from Langerdorf, Austria, to Ellis Island during the early part of the twentieth century, and worked in Chicago as a bartender in a Levee District speakeasy frequented by "Big Jim" Colosimo and Al Capone. Whenever federal agents would come to investigate the place, my grandfather flushed the hooch down the loo.

At night, from this high up, Chicago resembles a giant Lite-Brite board, but every so often, an angled street cuts through some of the illuminated squares. When I was in second grade at Daniel Boone Elementary School, Mrs. Schachter taught us that all the city's angled streets had once been Indian trails. Way down there on the West Side is one of them—Fifth Avenue. That's where Seymour Sidney Langer lived with his parents and his younger brother when he was growing up. He attended Penn Elementary School and Sumner Elementary; won a scholarship to take drawing classes at the Art Institute of Chicago; went to John Marshall High School with all the other first-generation kids of Yiddish-speaking immigrants on the West Side.

Marshall High was the school where all the best and brightest Chicago Jews went, my dad told me—in his stories, just about everyone at Marshall turned out to be a war hero, a lawyer, or a doctor, like him; the basketball team went to State; Irv Ellis, our Mozart Street neighbor, played on the team; two of my dad's buddies had tryouts with the Chicago Cubs; there were talent shows written by future Hollywood scribes Larry Gelbart and Sheldon Keller. When my dad talked about the West Side, it always sounded like such a wonderful, vibrant place to grow up, so much more exciting than my West Rogers Park, but he never took me there, even after I asked—the neighborhood had changed, he'd say, everyone was gone. "Who'd want to go now? You could get yourself killed just driving by." Until I was old enough to drive and brave enough to go to the West Side by myself, I could only imagine what my father's youth had been like, even though it had taken place less than a half hour away from where I grew up.

I can see two parallel rows of streetlamps just south of the Loop; they're lighting up Martin Luther King Drive, which was called South Parkway back in the day when my dad's father ran a soda-pop factory on the South Side of the city. The company was called S & L Beverages—*L* for Langer, *S* for some guy named Segal.

My dad, who said his first language was Yiddish—even after I was born, he peppered his conversation with Yiddish words and epithets: *Vuss? Cock ihm ohn!*—worked in the pop factory as a boy, tallying accounts. My father told me brief stories about life in the factory: gun-toting union men demanding dues; a holdup, during which Troubles, the factory's dog, was shot; a lawsuit filed by Pepsi-Cola against S & L for manufacturing a product called Pep Cola—my father suggested the company rename its cola "Loyal Clown."

S & L didn't last long, though. My father blamed its demise on the fact that sugar became scarce and expensive during World War II, and the factory never recovered from the economic hit it took. Afterward, my grandfather returned to work as a trucker delivering Jewel soda water to stores.

Perhaps in the 1940s, if you were on a plane flying into Chicago and gazing out the window like I am now, you could have seen the sparks from the streetcars my father rode from the West Side to downtown Chicago while he was still in high school and worked nights and weekends at the old *Chicago American* newspaper pasting up display advertisements. But the last Chicago streetcars stopped running long before I was born. And in the thirty-eight years of my life when my father was alive, I never took any streetcar or even any train or bus with him—only a car, a taxi, and once in a while an airplane. When I was a kid, my dad would drive north to Howard Street, where we'd sit in his car and watch trains coming in and out of the CTA yards, but we never got on any of them. I'd just sit on his front passenger seat, no seat belt. Sometimes, he'd let me sit on his lap and help him steer.

Below me, tiny cars speed east and west on some West Side boulevard. That's probably Roosevelt Road, with the long-ago-demolished vaudeville houses and Yiddish theaters where my father used to go with his high school buddies. And that dark patch to the west could well be Waldheim Cemetery out in Forest Park, where Sam and Becky Langer are buried and where my dad and his brother, Jerome, used to go every Father's and Mother's Day. Becky Langer died before I was born, when my dad was still in medical school. And when Sam Langer died, I didn't go to his funeral; in fact, I didn't even figure out he had died until several years afterward. Although one of my dad's favorite pastimes was thumbing through the obituaries in *The Chicago Daily News* and the *Tribune*, death was a topic he usually left out of the stories he told me. It took a trip to the dictionary for me to learn what my father meant when he said his uncle Harry Bell had long since "met his demise." And as far as Sam

Langer's *demise* is concerned, the only reason I know he died in 1974 is that once I saw on my dad's desk a note from a Jewish funeral home reminding him to light a Yizkor candle on the date of his father's death.

Even when my dad's father was alive, I never saw much of "Sam" anyway—my dad never referred to his father as "Dad" or "Pop" or "Pa," as my mother called her late father, Abe Herstein, an inventor who died before I was born and is probably worthy of a book of his own; it was always "Sam." An 8-mm film my father made of his dad was labeled simply "SAM." Sometimes, I would watch from a distance as my dad gave Sam a shave with a Norelco electric razor, but I never heard Sam tell any of his stories, never heard him discuss delivering pop, pouring bootleg liquor, serving in World War I, or being related to a general who fought for the Polish army. All I can remember is Sam living with his second wife, Rose, who pinched my cheek too hard and said "nowadays" and *"shayna punim"* a lot, in an apartment east of California Avenue on North Shore, then later in a nursing home near Lake Michigan. My dad never took me to visit him there—he was "in a bad way," my mother would explain, meaning, I learned much later, that he had had a stroke, had lost the ability to speak, and was suffering from depression.

Over the airplane's PA system, the flight attendant announces connecting gate information: "The Atlanta flight will leave from Gate B7 . . . For those of you traveling to Boston . . . If you are traveling to Urbana-Champaign . . ."

My dad went to college at the University of Illinois in Urbana-Champaign, where he boasted of being chugalug champion of Newman Hall and of befriending future NBC television personality Gene Shalit, who had a column in the *Daily Illini* called "What Shalit Be?" My dad finished college in two years, he said; classes were so easy that he loaded up on his courses to graduate as fast as he could.

We're zooming over Uptown now on the North Side of the city, where my dad lived in a room in his uncle Harry Bell's New Lawrence Hotel, a 1920s Art Deco building just east of the storied Aragon Ballroom, when he was attending the U of I medical school in Chicago. Uncle Harry was one of my father's relatives who made it big, a man who, in my dad's tales, brought to mind Uncle Ben in *Death of a Salesman*. ("Why, boys, when I was seventeen I walked into the jungle, and when I was twenty-one I walked out. And by God I was rich.") My dad told me that Uncle Harry owned not just the New Lawrence in Chicago but also the Edgewater in Madison, Wisconsin. A big man, my dad's uncle Harry, and my father spoke of him in the same respectful tones that he used to describe my cousin Sam Berkman, who, my father told us, invented the formula for Kayo chocolate drink and later started Bio-Science Laboratories, then became chairman of the board of Dow Chemical. My father liked to tell stories about the important and colorful people to whom we were related—not only the Polish general but Governor William Langer of North Dakota; also, Izzy Tuchman, a bread baker with supposedly Communist leanings who spoke on a soapbox at Chicago's legendary Bughouse Square.

We continue our descent, and there is the medical campus of the University of Illinois, once the site of West Side Park, where the Chicago Cubs played baseball before moving to Wrigley Field. And right over there is the Illinois Neuropsychiatric Institute (INI), which loomed over West Side Park's left field wall; it's where the phrase "out in left field" comes from. It's also where my mom worked for a time. Esther Herstein was a West Sider, too, and she and her twin sister, Eleanor, were the youngest of four children, still living with "Ma and Pa" near Garfield Park. My mom, a private, energetic woman with a passion for artists, particularly Paul Robeson, Laurence Olivier, and Orson Welles, was working as a secretary in the social services department at the University of Illinois when she met my dad, and she has told me that back then, my father briefly sported a Fu Manchu mustache and smoked cigarettes; he looked like "a real creep," she once joked. The Seymour Sidney Langer my mother described was a bon vivant—dated a lady ambulance driver nicknamed "Puppy Dog," held women's waists while they hula-hooped at one party, broke into the liquor cabinet at another. A much more vivacious man than the one I thought I knew. Before I was born, my dad owned a series of convertible Thunderbirds. But when I knew him, just about every car he owned was a black Ford hardtop sedan—they intimidated people because Chicago cops used them as unmarked cars; passersby would look in, see the man with the crew cut, wonder if maybe he was an undercover cop. The dad I knew seemed to like when people mistook him for someone else.

My mother and father married in 1952 at the Orrington Hotel in Evanston, Illinois. Their early days, from the stories they told me, consisted of trips to New York, of dinners at supper clubs with other couples, of evenings spent at South Side clubs like Club DeLisa and Near North nightspots such as Mister Kelly's. On a high shelf in my parents' basement is their honeymoon scrapbook; the cover is frayed and the pages are yellowed and brittle.

And now, *whooooosh,* here we are flying above Michigan Avenue, the city's Magnificent Mile, where my dad worked in the sixties and seventies as a radiologist in private practice, reading the X-rays of such patients as Hugh Hefner and the first Mayor Richard Daley, and where he used to take me on Saturday mornings while my mother was at the beauty parlor. We'd walk into the office in darkness. He liked being there when no one else was, but I'd never feel safe until he turned on the lights. Yes, there's the site of Health Research Associates, where Dr. Seymour Sidney Langer taught me to recognize a normal chest, tuberculosis, and diverticulitis, and for a time inspired me to want to become a radiologist just like him. He read X-rays at warp speed—one, then the next, up the film went on the light box, down on the desk, an artistic but illegible scribble on a piece of paper, back into the manila envelope, on to the next X-ray, until he was done and could set the pile aside. But 720 N. Michigan was torn down in the 1980s, replaced by a condo building and Saks Fifth Avenue. My dad's next office, three blocks down at the Marriott Hotel, is gone now, too, and so is the Life Extension Institute, for which he worked before he joined the University of Illinois faculty and medical staff full-time.

My father loved his job, said so all the time. Radiology was like detective work—you could tell nearly everything about a person by looking at his X-ray. At the family dinner table, he would tell short stories he had gleaned from clues on this or that film: a bullet wound, a butterfly clasp on a brassiere, a hint of old tuberculosis. My father discussed TB with respect and admiration, as if the disease were his archrival—Sherlock Holmes talking about Professor Moriarty. He even seemed disappointed when TB was more or less eradicated in the United States. Sanitariums should remain open, perhaps for AIDS patients, perhaps if TB came back—this was one of his theories. A secret plan should be hatched to fake an invasion from Mars so that the United States and the Soviet Union could join forces against a common enemy, and thus end the Cold War—that was another Seymour Sidney Langer theory.

The plane curbs left, and looking out the window across the aisle, I can glimpse East Rogers Park, where my dad and mom lived in an apartment on Lunt Avenue, right by the lake, and where their first two children—my brother, Bradley, and sister, Karen—lived before the family moved west. And there, in that grid of pink lights, is West Rogers Park, where the five of us lived in the house my parents bought in 1960, the only house they ever owned, the house where my mother still lives, a three-bedroom, two-story red-and-brown brick Georgian that my father once told me was the biggest one on our block, but which, I later discovered, was really no bigger than most of the others.

I was born in 1967, and when I lived with my parents, I sensed that any struggles my mother and father may have had were part of the past. My parents' old neighborhood served mostly as material for their wistful or romantic lore—they'd talk about sleeping in Garfield Park at night in the summer after the air-cooled movie palaces had closed, watching dancers on the rooftops of West Side apartment buildings, riding the streetcar downtown to the Loop or to Oak Street Beach. The world my parents had left behind seemed a distant, airbrushed memory—idyllic and romantic, yet so far away.

At times, I'd envy the journey they had taken. Every weekday morning when I was growing up, my father would awake at five and head out to work. He would arrive home sometime after one, nap, read, come down in time for dinner. At the Langer dinner table—my mother didn't return to work until I was in high school, and she always prepared dinner—he'd listen to classical music or BBC word-game shows. Over dinner, he'd tell us how many X-rays he'd read, how quickly he'd read them, and as he grew older, how the medical profession was becoming little more than bean counting; the artistry of it had gone to hell.

On weekend nights, there were dinners at the Cape Cod Room, Miller's, the Blue Peacock, or Myron & Phil's. My dad liked being a regular at restaurants, liked knowing maître d's and waiters, calling them by name ("How're you doin', Umberto?"), liked guessing their nationalities ("Ecuadorian?"). He liked estimating how much meals would cost and guessing right most of the time; when he guessed too high, he'd say he would still be right if you figured in the tip. On some Friday nights or Sunday afternoons, we'd attend Chicago Symphony concerts, conducted by Sir Georg Solti, my father's favorite because Solti worked fast—if he started conducting at 8:00 P.M., chances were that you could be back to your car by 9:30.

Perhaps this was not the most captivating and adventurous existence a kid could have imagined, but I could rely on it. Ditto for my relationship with my dad, a man I respected and admired but around whom I rarely felt at ease. I feared his judgment, his ability with a look or syllable to make me feel like a fool. He seemed to already know everything I knew, also why what I knew wasn't worth knowing. I'd make a joke and he'd stare blankly—he liked to call himself "the Great Stone Face." "I don't get it," he'd say. Around my father, I'd feel guilty for acting too immature; around my mother, guilty for growing up too quickly.

Being born the youngest child by far in a family of five can sometimes feel like walking into a movie a half hour after it has begun—something my father did often when I was a kid, before he stopped going to movies altogether. Who knew why he didn't like to show up at the beginning. So he wouldn't have to fight for a place to park? So he wouldn't have to feel controlled by someone else's schedule? So no one in the theater would see him walking in or walking out, or walking at all?

At least when you walked into movies late with my parents, though, you could stay past the ending and wait for the movie to start over to see what you had missed, wait for the moment you'd walked into the middle of *Return of the Pink Panther* or *The Last of the Red Hot Lovers* or *Day for Night.* The same does not hold true in a family. By the time I was in kindergarten, my sister was already in high school and my brother was attending college in Canada, and what may or may not have happened before my arrival ("You must have been a mistake," grade school wags said) was something I had to piece together through what I saw and through the stories my family members told me.

Much of my youth was spent figuring out what I probably should have already known. "Has he seen a doctor about his appendages?" my pediatrician, Dr. Steiner, once asked my mother sotto voce with reference to me; my mother responded with characteristic brevity and understated drama, "Yes, but nothing can be done." That was another story my dad had neglected to tell me, something I had to figure out for myself.

I knew early on that my father walked differently from most people, but I understood, too, that this was something one didn't discuss. My grade school pal David would ask, "Why does your father walk like that?" and I would shush him—*No, you don't ask that.* It took years for me to realize that the way he walked—toes pointed inward, rolling from side to side—was in any way related to the fact that I was so lousy in gym class, barely able to tread water, always one of the last to finish the six-hundred-yard dash, last or second-to-last boy picked for kick baseball.

The realization came accidentally. Since the age of five, I had been taking piano lessons with Alice Schwartzberg, a stern but kind Austrian Jew who drove a green Buick Electra and wore glasses on a chain. She escaped from Europe during the war and taught piano to both me and my sister, either at our house or in her East Rogers Park apartment, where my mother sat and read *The New Yorker* and occasionally sampled Mrs. Schwartzberg's dietetic candies while I stumbled through scales, études, and sonatas. But when I was in middle school, Mrs. Schwartzberg and her husband, Ben, moved to an apartment in Lakeview. It was in an elevator building with a hallway that had perpetual mirrors, which showed me for the first time the way I moved—feet pointed inward, slightly rolling from one side to the other, just like, or at least pretty similar to, my dad.

But I was not convinced that I would always walk this way. I tried to overcome it by walking in a manner unlike my father's. I pointed my feet outward, took short, quick steps, monitored my gait, readjusted whenever I passed my reflection in Mrs. Schwartzberg's building. I resented anyone who had the effrontery to call attention to my inherited handicap, especially anybody who referred to it as such—not so much one high school thespian who offered the nickname "Crazy Legs"; more so a schmuck who auditioned for a high school production of *A Thousand Clowns* along with me and who declared that no director would ever cast someone who *walked like that;* also, a potbellied wiseass who rented out his porno mags to the future attorney and screenwriter in our debate class and called out "Yo, Limp-Laig!" whenever he saw me; my father most of all, who never prepared me for these remarks, never actually mentioned my condition to me, only referred to it vaguely while suggesting what size and kind of shoes I should buy or while filling out physical exam forms before I went to high school—"Ability to run and jump is limited," he wrote—but as for the specifics of my dysplasia, the X-rays of which were eventually taken by another doctor, I didn't discuss these issues with my dad, who seemed to be considerably more affected by his hip condition than I ever was by mine.

No, ours was not a wonderfully loving and open relationship, but at the same time, it was rarely fraught with great tension. It was a typical relationship between a Depression-era father and son. My dad and I shook hands; we didn't hug. *Love* was not a word in our vocabulary; I don't recall my father uttering it except when he discussed how he felt about being a radiologist or when he was quoting song lyrics: "Betty Co-ed is *loved* by every college boy." But, though I may have flipped him off behind his back once or twice from the backseat of one of his Fords when I was nine, I did so more out of boredom and curiosity than from any actual anger, using the new gesture a fellow student had taught me, feeling empowered by its eloquence. I yelled at him only once, one more time than he ever raised his voice to me, but by then, I was in my late thirties and he was drugged up on OxyContin and was refusing medical attention for what he claimed was a series of TIAs (transient ischemic attacks). I felt bad for yelling at him, felt worse that he seemed to respect me more after I'd done it.

But there were never any games of catch or fishing trips, no heartfelt talks between Pop and Junior, no late-night rap sessions about girls or sex or God, no great words of wisdom or lessons ("Just keep doin' what you're doin'; you're doin' fine," he'd say, whether I was doing well or not). On the few occasions when my dad took on the role of father, I had trouble taking him seriously; his behavior seemed so uncharacteristic—for example, his brief admonishment to me in high school for having dialed a recorded telephone sex line ("I asked the operator what these calls were for, and she started *laughin'* "); his one aborted attempt to teach me how to drive his car ("You're gettin' too close to that goddamn curb!").

When I was a child and my siblings were in their teens, my father seemed happy to turn the child-rearing duties over to them, along with my mother, and I often felt as if I were being raised as the only child of four parents. The less my dad traveled, the more trips I took with my mom and sister. My brother was only in his early twenties when he took my mom and me to Belgium and France, while my dad stayed at home. What did my dad do while we were gone? Stayed home, I assumed, read books, bought cold cuts from the Romanian deli and Meyer's Delicatessen, went to work, came home, ate dinner with my sister or alone, the way I always imagined him most content.

My father and I bantered more than we talked, Seymour Langer's conversations with me consisting mostly of witticisms, of quotations, both of famous personages and himself, glib, smart-alecky proclamations that often served the purpose of ending conversations: "Frankly, it's been better in the past"; "Evi*dent*ly"; "So where's this alleged dinner?"; "The reason stated is never the reason." Or, in the words he borrowed from Charlie Chaplin in *The Great Dictator*, commenting upon a faulty parachute, "Far from perfect."

My father wouldn't talk on the phone to his relatives; he'd "chew the fat." He'd begin conversations with "How the hell are ya?" and wind them up with "In any event . . ." He'd invent silly neologisms and pronunciations. You wouldn't *throw a ball;* you'd *trunn* one. A butterfly was a *flutterby;* strawberries were *strummeries.* How much did something cost? *Eleventy-two* dollars. He regaled waiters with Mark Twain quotes or his favorite John Barrymore riposte to a coughing spectator: "Throw that walrus a fish!" Occasionally, a line from Shakespeare would find its way into his conversation. In 1980, I was searching *Bartlett's Familiar Quotations* for pithy phrases to insert into my Bar Mitzvah speech, and my dad suggested this line from *Julius Caesar:* "The fault, dear Brutus, is not in our stars / But in ourselves, that we are underlings." I had no idea what the words meant, and, no, my father never explained why he liked them. But I put them in the speech anyway.

I never did get much closer to him. Even when he would burst into song, he would offer only snippets of a larger story: "*Tangerine*," he'd sing, then stop; "K-K-K-Katy"; "Bingo, Bango, Bongo, I don't want to leave the Congo"; "Who's your little who-zis"; and later, eerily, in the last snippet of a song I ever heard him sing, when he was trying out a new tape recorder I had bought for him, "We three, we're all alone," from the Ink Spots song "We Three (My Echo, My Shadow, and Me)."

"Welcome to Chicago," one of the flight attendants says.

II

At my O'Hare arrival gate, I can see my dim reflection in the window. In a stationary position, I resemble my mother; in motion, I favor my father. From my dad, I have inherited hazel eyes; a caustic sense of humor; an intense focus and an urge to complete projects quickly; a degenerative hip condition; a profound distrust of religious, political, and medical institutions; and a taste for pickled herring, Chinese food, and the works of S. J. Perelman.

My dad gave me my first sport coat (red-white-and-blue-checked), my first bike (the yellow Schwinn), my first car (a gray 1988 Ford Escort). But in terms of material but nonpractical items, my father never gave me many gifts. My dad wasn't much better at giving gifts than he was at receiving them. "This is a tie," he'd say while shaking a box to guess its contents, before he'd add, "which I don't want." "This is a belt, *and I already have a belt*." "This is a sweater, *and I don't wear sweaters*." Which made the few items he did give me all the more meaningful—most were stamps and coins: proof sets from the U.S. Treasury, first-day covers of U.S. stamps, and his 1930 Junior Postage Album, the only artifact I still have from my father's childhood.

The stamp album is a hefty hardbound volume, thick as a dictionary, with a frayed navy blue cover with gold-embossed letters. Inside are thousands of stamps that my father, when he was a kid, affixed in their squares. Slipped between various pages like leaves pressed and preserved in a memory book are envelopes postmarked in the 1930s and addressed to one of my father's boyhood homes. Shortly before he died, I asked my father why he had given me his stamp album—I had been hoping for some long-sought-after statement of father-son love, for some clue about who he was before I knew him. "For the hell of it," he said. The conversation ended there.

Here at O'Hare, as I wait for my connecting flight, I think about how this will be the first time I'll pass through Chicago without stopping at home. But when I check the departures monitor, I notice that my flight has been canceled. "Weather in New York," the gate agent tells me. The next New York–bound plane won't take off until 6:00 A.M. I put on my backpack and head out into the winter night, bound for the taxis.

"Mozart Street. West Rogers Park," I tell the driver.

And now I find myself heading east on the Kennedy Expressway. I make a quick call to my mom to tell her I'll be stopping by and staying over tonight.

My mother begins to say something, then stops.

"What?" I ask.

There is a pause. To me, my mother's pauses have always seemed freighted with meaning, but in the years of my father's illness and now afterward, even more so.

"What?" I ask again.

"When you get here, I'll show you," she says.

"What's that?"

Another pause.

"Something of Dad's."

My mother, Esther Langer, tends to endow even seemingly innocuous phrases with grave import. I've joked with her that she can sound like a character out of either a Harold Pinter or a Eugene O'Neill play. When I was eight, my mom's favorite porcelain cookie container, adorned with cheerful pictures of geese and the phrase "Goosey Goosey Gander," fell off our refrigerator and shattered. My mom didn't cry or yell. She just looked down, shook her head, sighed. "No more Goosey Goosey Gander," she said, and I still remember how crestfallen I felt at her understatement, how much I wanted to gather up the pieces of the container and put them back together. Shortly after his retirement, my dad was asleep upstairs while my mother and I were in the living room watching the Ingmar Bergman movie *The Silence*. In the film, a woman named Ester is suffering from an unspecified disease, and while she lies in bed, her young nephew ventures out into the hallway of their hotel and happens upon a troupe of circus dwarves. Looking at the dwarves, my mother remarked, "They're the lucky ones; they're only deformed on the outside." Not long afterward, when my father was housebound, my mother and I were standing on her front porch. A plane passed overhead. "Look at that plane," she said wistfully. "Some people are going places."

When you get here, I'll show you. . . . Something of Dad's.

"I'll be there soon," I tell my mom.

Cabdrivers have rarely known how to get to my parents' house, so I quickly rattle off precise directions for the route my father always took. My dad was proud of how well he knew this city, its shortcuts, its streets with names like Archer, Ogden, and Narragansett; he drove fast with two feet—one on the gas, one on the brakes.

I tell my driver to head east on the Kennedy, exit right at Nagle, go east on Devon, and take Devon past Caldwell Woods, all the way into the city. Turn left and head north on California Avenue, I say, take another left on North Shore, past K.I.N.S., the synagogue where I attended High Holiday services with my dad until he stopped going to shul altogether. Then I say to make one final left onto Mozart Street and stop at the house with the handicapped parking sign out front; it's still there, even though my father is not.

In the taxi, my driver laughs when he hears where I'm going. He lives in Rogers Park and says he rarely gets any passengers who aren't businesspeople or tourists going straight downtown. We talk awhile, and he tells me he's from Haiti. He was studying agriculture in Paris when François Duvalier took power in 1957, and came to Chicago when he felt he could no longer return home because his life would be threatened there.

I ask the driver if he has ever considered leaving Chicago.

"I've been trying to leave Chicago for fifty years," he says.

III

When I get out of the cab, I can see a light on in an upstairs bedroom. My mother, as seems always to be the case now, must still be awake. Almost eighty, she keeps an intimidatingly active schedule: staying up late, getting up early, exercising, taking English literature classes at Northeastern Illinois University. She often speaks of how brilliant my dad was, how quickly he could read books, but she reads more than any of us ever did, still powers through the works of Thackeray, Hardy, Conrad, Dickens. She's always talked about how fast my father did everything, but hers is the energy I've often had trouble matching.

I walk toward the front of the house, past my mother's frozen garden and up to the stoop where my dad used to sit on a lawn chair while I sat on the steps. I lived in this house for the first seventeen years of my life; I came back home after college and lived here for another year, came over for dinner an average of twice a week until I was in my early thirties, when my father's stays at the dinner table became ever briefer, his unspoken effort, it always seemed to me, to let the family run its course and to let his children go their own ways:

"How long are you stayin'?" he'd ask whenever I arrived. "Are you gonna be sleepin' here? Are you on your way in or on your way out?"

During all that time here, I hardly knew a day when my father wasn't home by early afternoon. He never took business trips, never took vacation time; even during the great blizzard of 1967, half a year before I was born, when the snows rendered Mozart Street impassable, he trudged down these steps in his fawn-colored fur-lined boots, bound for the Morse Avenue elevated train station. Every night I slept here, he was sleeping in the bed across the hall; every time I was here for dinner, so was he. There he would be, at the head of the kitchen or dining room table, upstairs in his bed reading John Keegan or Samuel Eliot Morison, in the living room watching the Bears game on TV, looking out the window to see if my brother or sister was coming home. I can imagine my father in every room of this house. I can see the artworks he made—the collages and sculptures in the basement, the paintings of animals on the laundry room heating pipes, the pencil drawings of the Chicago skyline in the living room. Strange that he won't be in any of those rooms when I walk inside; this house always seemed to be so much his domain. I'd walk into the kitchen and open the refrigerator. "Why don't you open the refrigerator?" he'd say. I'd pour myself a glass of juice; then he'd say, "Why don't you take a glass of juice?"

I open the screen door. *Why don't you open the screen door?* I take out my house keys. *You comin' in or goin' out?* But as I enter the front hallway, it's my mother's voice I hear coming from upstairs.

"Ad, is that you?"

"It's me," I say. "I'll be right there."

I take off my backpack and shoes, hang up my jacket in the front closet, where my dad used to hang his suit jackets and doctor's coats. I pour myself a glass of water in the kitchen, where he used to sit in the only armchair. *Why don't you take a glass of water?* The house seems utterly quiet and cold. I walk past the dining room, where my dad led Passover seders, blazing through the Haggadah until he got to the part about the "festival meal," zipping upstairs to bed after dinner with barely a good night or a goodbye. I gaze into the den, with its dingy burnt-orange carpet that my mother hated but my dad bought anyway; the Duraflame logs are even now still in their brown wrapping paper for the fireplace that he never wanted to use. "Another day, Esther," he'd tell my mother, "another day." The door that leads to the back porch is locked tonight. Out there is my father's motorized wheelchair, and past it, the door that gives onto an electric mini-elevator that took him up and down when he could no longer walk the stairs.

"Ad?" my mother calls down.

"Be right there."

On the second floor are three bedrooms and two bathrooms. In my sister's old bedroom are drawings and sketches my dad made; in the aqua-walled bedroom that I shared with my brother when I was old enough to sleep in my own bed are my old pictures on the wall and my *Quadrophenia* poster on the door and a snow globe atop the dresser, and the bed from which, just two months ago, I was awakened by the sound of a phone ringing, then my mother's voice, then her footsteps approaching. I knew what she would say before she told me.

In my parents' old room, my mother's glasses are off as she sits at my father's desk, looking at papers under a fluorescent lamp. She gets up when I enter the room, and we embrace. How long has it been since I was last here? Two months and a lifetime. How did Michael Caine put it in one of my mother's and my favorite movies, *The Man Who Would Be King*? "Three summers and a thousand years ago."

"I'll show you. What I was telling you about." She takes a piece of paper from the pile on the desk and hands it to me. "I found it in the letter tray."

The letter tray was where my dad kept pictures, greeting cards, and, later, get-well cards. But I don't recognize the brief letter my mother gives me—it was written by the Pulitzer Prize–winning historian Barbara Tuchman, author of *The Guns of August* and *The Zimmerman Telegram,* books my dad often urged me to read. The letter is dated February 12, 1982.

"Dear Dr. Langer," the letter reads, "I think the Bonus March would make a great story. Good luck and thank you for your kind words."

"That is somethin' else, isn't it? How about that?" my mother says. "You remember the Bonus March, Ad? You remember that one?"

Of course I do.

The Bonus March was a relatively obscure but pivotal event that took place in my father's boyhood during the Great Depression. As my dad told the story, a federal law had been passed in 1924 entitling veterans of World War I additional payment for their service—$1.00 for every day served at home, $1.25 for every day overseas—but that money was not payable until 1945 or until a veteran's death. In the early 1930s, during the depths of the Depression, poverty-stricken veterans, fearing their money wouldn't come until after they died, lobbied Washington, where Texas congressman Wright Patman sponsored a bill calling for immediate payment. Approximately twenty thousand veterans of World War I, in which my dad said my grandfather had served, massed in Washington, D.C. Known as the Bonus Army or the Bonus Expeditionary Force (B.E.F.), the vets marched around the nation's Capitol, camped out for the better part of two months along the banks of the Anacostia River and elsewhere throughout D.C., continued to camp and picket even after their bonus bill was soundly defeated in the Senate, until a bloody confrontation, which left two marchers dead. Then, President Hoover called in Gen. Douglas MacArthur and members of the U.S. cavalry, who fought their own veterans and forced them out with tear gas, rifles, and bayonets.

For more than thirty years, my father talked about writing a history of the Bonus March. The most overlooked incident in twentieth-century American history, he called it, a time when the country was on the verge of a coup d'état. It was an event that history books had left out, but one that should be remembered. He talked about the need he felt to preserve the memory of the generation that had been neglected by its own government; he talked about the need to remember the Bonus March even as he was beginning to lose his own memory.

You remember the Bonus March, Ad? You remember that one?

I do.

The Bonus March book was far from the only project my father discussed but never completed. There was the painting of a female nude, for which he'd drawn sketches; a fountain he would build for our backyard. Often, he would discuss plans, then never mention them again. "When you get back from Disney World, maybe we'll think about getting a dog." "When you head off to college, we'll buy an old station wagon, drive it cross-country, leave it there so you can use it." He talked about buying a liquor store downtown and running it with my brother; opening a frame shop and having my sister run it; opening a pastry shop, where my mom could work with the wife of one of his high school buddies. There was the real estate he might buy in Wisconsin, the apartment on the Magnificent Mile, the ranch house around the block. Most of these projects were mentioned no more than once or twice—you'd bring them up again with my dad and he'd shoot you a quizzical and dismissive glance, like a drunk with a hangover being reminded of the trouble he'd caused the night before.

My father was not a writer. To my knowledge, his published work consists only of the occasional coauthored medical paper and letters to the *American Journal of Roentgenology*. But the Bonus March book was the one project he never stopped talking about. In 1970 or 1971, when my brother was a student at Mather High School and looking for topics for a U.S. history research paper, my dad helped him write one about the Bonus March; the paper is still on one of my parents' bookshelves. More than ten years later, my father wrote to Barbara Tuchman about it.

You remember the Bonus March?

I can remember my dad dictating to my mother "Author's Query" letters to *The New York Times Book Review,* asking if any surviving witnesses to the Bonus March could help with the book he wanted to write. My mother typed them up and sent them to the paper. During lulls in conversation, my dad would return to the topic: "Have I ever told you about the Bonus March?" Whenever I had trouble coming up with an idea for a high school report, he'd say, "Have you thought about researching the Bonus March?"

Sometimes at the dinner table, all of us would talk about the trip he would take to West Branch, Iowa, to visit the Herbert Hoover Presidental Library—that's where, he said, he'd conduct his research. Maybe he'd fly to Iowa, or maybe he'd drive; he never seemed sure. He would ask my mother to assemble lists of hotels there. I always got excited when he discussed his book. And the fact that my dad didn't write it seemed, and still seems, to me like some small tragedy, a sign that his life was incomplete. Maybe if he'd had other interests, I'd often think, maybe if he'd continued to pursue his art, maybe if he'd written his book . . . His life always seemed equally divided between medical offices and the house on Mozart Street; I liked the idea of there being more to it.

I never learned all that much about the Bonus March, but toward the end of my dad's life, the book seemed like a project we might work on together. When I was a kid, we collaborated on art projects—movies, stories, sculptures. Those are some of my best memories of my dad, but what I remember most about them is that, like the stories he told, they rarely lasted long, and that my father would begin projects but wouldn't see them through. We worked together on a Super 8 adaptation of one of my favorite books, Jane Thayer's *The Blueberry Pie Elf,* in which I starred as the titular elf, sampling blueberries from a giant pie my father had made out of foam rubber. I had such a good time making this movie, hamming it up for the camera, jumping up and down on the foam rubber, that I was eager to make another, to adapt Betty Yurdin's book *The Tiger in the Teapot*. But even though my dad made the tiger costume for me, we never shot the movie—he finally took slides of me dressed as a tiger, emerging from a giant green garbage drum, which, to me, seemed wholly inadequate.

My father once said that he and I should read the dictionary together, write down lists of words on slips of paper, learn a certain number per week, but we didn't get past the first page of the *A*'s— we started with *aardvark*, ended with *abrasion*. Sometimes I would lie on his bed with my head on his chest and listen to him read aloud from Samuel Eliot Morison's *Oxford History of the American People*, but that is the only book I can recall the two of us reading together. He'd talk to me of collaborating on a children's book, *The Secret Sicilian Salami Society*, but after finishing a chapter, he lost interest in this project, too. I tried continuing the story on my own but didn't get far writing the story myself seemed wrong. And eventually, we stopped working on any artistic projects together.

When I was an adult and had embarked on a career as a writer and editor, and walking became more difficult for my father, we would talk about my going to Iowa to research the Bonus March for him. I could take notes, I'd say, xerox files, bring them back to Chicago. Later, my mother would ask me to teach my dad to navigate the Internet so he could research his book from home.

When my father retired from medicine in the autumn of 2002, he did so with little fanfare. He came home from work early in the afternoon, as always, and went upstairs to bed early, too. Though my dad was well into his seventies, my mother and I assumed this would be the beginning of the time he would follow through on the projects he had always wanted to complete; he could paint, he could draw, and now he could finally write his Bonus March book.

Instead, what happened was a long, slow decline, as if he had already lost both his will and his patience. I'd show him photographs or videos I'd taken; he'd walk out of the room midway through. My mother and I would give him books; he wouldn't finish reading them. We'd still talk about the Bonus Army, but now when I would mention researching the book, it seemed to have acquired the same fantasy aspect that characterized the new projects he had begun to discuss, such as calling up Gene Shalit and asking if he could help me restart the defunct *Punch* magazine. ("But Dad, starting a magazine costs a lot of money," I said. "I've *got* money," he replied. "No, Dad, I mean a *lot* of money.") Frequently, when I would talk to my father, I would still offer to go to the Hoover Library. "No, I'll go there myself when I feel like it," he'd say, but by then, I think we both knew that he wouldn't make it out of town. When he died on November 2, 2005, as far as I know, he hadn't written a word of his book. Even his "Author's Query" requests to *The New York Times Book Review* were never published.

I never found out why the Bonus March was the one historical incident that seemed to interest him more than any other. Perhaps he wanted to write about it because his father was a veteran of World War I and, like many other veterans, felt marginalized when he returned. Could my grandfather Sam Langer actually have gone to Washington, D.C., to protest with his brethren? Could my dad have gone with him? Did the fact that my father was physically unable to serve in the military make him that much more concerned with veterans' issues? Did the symbolism of a march have particular resonance for a man who had difficulty walking?

"That Rosebud you're trying to find out about— Maybe that was something he lost," says a character in *Citizen Kane,* my mother's favorite film, in which a dying man's last word, spoken to a snow globe, leads to a search for that man's history and identity. Maybe the Bonus March represented something my father had lost.

"That book would have been somethin' else," my mother says. "Your father, he was somethin' else."

Before my mother and I head downstairs to continue our conversation, I ask if I can make a copy of the Barbara Tuchman letter. She looks uncertain, as if not knowing what I might have in mind. But she nods, then asks how long I'll be staying.

Barely overnight, I tell her—I have to catch a 6:00 A.M. flight.

IV

There are some unexpected advantages to growing up with a distant father, one who often substituted clever quips for deep conversation, who usually left what he might have been thinking or feeling up to the imagination. You learn to rely on your instincts and to trust your own judgment. And yet you wonder what you might have missed out on. You wonder why you felt so disconnected at the funeral that sometimes it seemed to you as if you were only watching yourself there, not actually participating. You wonder why you didn't cry. You wonder if the grief will hit you later, the way you've often heard grief described. But you wonder, too, if you might wind up not feeling it at all. And you regret this, too.

It's just after 4:00 A.M. and I'm in another cab, this time heading away from my mother's house en route to O'Hare Airport. In my backpack, I have a copy of the letter that Barbara Tuchman wrote to my father; it's tucked between pages of the high school paper my brother wrote about the Bonus March.

The taxi driver hasn't said much, and neither have I. It's too early to talk anyway, and I have more than enough to occupy my mind. I'm thinking about my father's Bonus March book. The project seems symbolic of my relationship with my dad—something that could have taught me more about him and his generation, something that might have brought us together but was left unfinished. The book he never wrote is the story of what we didn't do together, of the conversations we didn't have, of the projects we didn't finish, of the stories he left out, of the inner life, about which I knew so little, of what our relationship could have been but wasn't. And the Bonus March itself reminds me of the relationship between a searching child and a detached father, a quixotic effort to collect on some debt.

My taxi driver is continuing to speed west on Devon, a route that's different from the one I usually take. But that's okay. For taxi drivers, while navigating the way to my parents' house can sometimes be difficult, getting away from it and finding the airport has never been a problem. For me, the opposite has always been true—like my father, I've always had trouble leaving Chicago behind. But when I finally do get inside O'Hare, look up at a departures monitor, and find my flight, I see that it's the first one of the day. And it's right on time.

Stories We Tell

Strange, isn't it? Each man's life touches so many other lives.

THE ANGEL CLARENCE, *It's a Wonderful Life*

1971

It seems appropriate that the most dramatic event in my relationship with my father might be one that I can't actually remember happening.

My father often spoke of the power of his memory, and, aside from this particular incident, my memories, too, tend to be particularly vivid. Memories of my childhood include the smell of dead alewives on Lunt Avenue Beach, where I would walk and swim with my mother, and the taste of the crunchy kichels and the swirled reddish chocolate cupcakes we'd buy at Knopov's Bakery on Devon Avenue. I can remember when I still had a playpen in my family's den, and I would lie in it and watch my stuffed red terry-cloth elephant twirl above me. I can remember scents: my father's lemon-lime aftershave, Johnson's baby shampoo long before the formula was changed, Poly-Vi-Sol liquid vitamins before I was old enough to chew, Crayolas in Miss O'Connor's kindergarten classroom. Zwieback biscuits are my madeleine. But I don't remember this story happening; it's the first one I know about me and my father, and I only know it because I heard it so often as a child.

The story takes place in a Sheridan Avenue barbershop in East Rogers Park, across the street from the 400 Theater, which had two-person love seats, in which my father liked to sit alone. Our barber there was Mr. Sobel; he was a nice-enough man, but I never enjoyed seeing him. I never liked how he pushed his thumbs against my ears to make me turn one way or another. I never liked the smell of his cigarettes. I never liked the feel of his coarse brush against my neck or the smell of the talcum powder he brushed me with. I especially hated the stories he told about the neighborhood, all of which seemed to involve scary men committing armed robbery.

"They hit the drugstore again," he'd say.

"Who?" my father would ask.

"Color guy," Mr. Sobel would respond.

Or he'd say, "They held me up."

"Who?"

"Color guys."

"What happened?"

"They got the cash register. The little guy, I took him and I threw him up against the wall, but the big guy, he put a knife to my throat. I told him, 'Take the register.' "

I was a shy, scared kid in general and was frightened of just about everything. Once, I heard a story on my father's car radio about a four-year-old kid on Clarendon Street answering his door and being shot dead, so whenever we'd pass the yellow-and-black Clarendon street sign, I'd dive down on the backseat of my dad's Ford. I cowered in the audience of the Carnegie Theater during a coming attraction for a new film called *Dirty Harry*. I felt scared of the Who's *Tommy* and the Beatles' *Revolver* albums, which my brother, Bradley, played on the eight-track of my dad's car. Sometimes, I felt scared of just talking to people, and viewed it as a point of pride if I could get through an entire haircut at Mr. Sobel's barbershop without uttering a word.

But because of the stories of holdups and robberies Mr. Sobel told about "color guys," whom I imagined as men with swirling, colorful faces, I spent my barbershop visits more quiet and terrified than I usually felt, waiting for the moment when robbers would break in and shoot me. I would sit in the maroon booster seat atop the cushion of the antique Theo A. Kochs barber's chair, a sheet around me, staring silently at my reflection, waiting for Mr. Sobel to finish so I could get back home.

On the day that the incident in question takes place, it's late afternoon when Mr. Sobel is done cutting my hair. He gives me a hard candy to suck on. Suddenly, it lodges in my throat. I start coughing. Soon, I can't breathe. I begin to turn blue. My father quickly grabs me, turns me upside down, shakes me up and down and up and down until the candy pops out.

"Your daddy saved your life. He picked you up and turned you upside down and shook you, and I said I'd never give candy to any kid again," Mr. Sobel frequently told me later to remind me of the incident that I had managed to block out. My father would never tell me this story, but my siblings and my mother often would recount this tale of my dad as my hero. But after that day, although I have distinct memories of the barbershop, I don't recall ever going back there with my father. In my mind's eye, my mother is the one who takes me there, while my dad stays at home.

ROSS McELWEE

I'm on the last leg of a train trip from New York to Boston, studying up on the Bonus March. My dad's right; it's quite a story, one that manages to condense an epic tale of the Depression-era America in which he grew up into one tragic summer in Washington, D.C. The story of the Bonus March also concerns the rise of both fascism and communism, when leftists infiltrated the Bonus Army and found themselves pitted against its increasingly right-wing leadership. It's the story, too, of the fall of Herbert Hoover and the rise of Franklin Roosevelt, as the routing of the Bonus Army helped turn public opinion against the Hoover administration.

The Bonus March is the *Zelig* of twentieth-century American historical incidents. It influenced both Martin Luther King, Jr., who credited the march with his 1968 plans to build a poor people's tent city across from the White House, and Senator John Kerry, who camped out in D.C. with other members of Vietnam Veterans Against the War in 1971. When he was advising President Nixon on how to deal with the protests of Vietnam vets, Pat Buchanan invoked the history of the Bonus vets.

The story is loaded with great characters, too. Not just Hoover and MacArthur, who were the ones my dad talked about, but also Gen. George S. Patton, who evicted a veteran named Joe Angelo, who had saved Patton's life during World War I, and Maj. Dwight D. Eisenhower, who served during the time of the march as assistant executive to the assistant secretary of war. And then there are marginal historical figures, whom my dad never talked about but who played pivotal roles nonetheless: Walter W. Waters, the unemployed Oregon laborer and veteran of World War I who became commander of the Bonus Expeditionary Force and later, as he began to identify with Benito Mussolini, the leader of a short-lived fascist party called the Khaki Shirts; Brig. Gen. Pelham D. Glassford, the flamboyant, boot-clad, motorcycle-riding D.C. police chief who served under MacArthur during World War I but who helped feed the marchers and served as their treasurer during the march, then resigned shortly after the marchers were forced out; Royal Robertson, an unemployed Hollywood actor, head of the Bonus Army's California contingent, who led a solemn nighttime "Death March" around the Capitol while wearing a neck brace.

My father maintained that the Bonus March was the most over-looked incident in twentieth-century American history. But there's still a lot of material out there. John Dos Passos wrote of the marchers' plight in his book *In All Countries;* Ernest Hemingway wrote about them in *To Have and Have Not.* The subject was also covered by onetime *New Republic* literary editor Malcolm Cowley in his memoir *Dream of the Golden Mountains,* by William Manchester in *The Glory and the Dream,* by Studs Terkel in *Hard Times,* and by H. L. Mencken, Will Rogers, and Gore Vidal. More recently, there was the 2004 book *The Bonus Army: An American Epic,* by Paul Dickson and Thomas B. Allen, and in the 2008 book *Give Me Liberty,* Naomi Wolf referenced the Bonus Army, asserting that George W. Bush's government would never allow another Bonus March to take place.

I've been listening to blues songs, such as Peetie Wheatstraw's "When I Get My Bonus (Things Will Be Coming My Way)." I've read two Bonus March–inspired novels: John D. Weaver's gripping *Another Such Victory* and William Almon Wolff's rightly forgotten *Murder at Endor.* I've watched the Bonus Army in Hollywood movies, such as *Washington Merry-Go-Round* and *Gold Diggers of 1933,* in which Joan Blondell paid them and their generation tribute in the song "My Forgotten Man." And I've watched the peculiar 1933 feature film *Gabriel Over the White House,* starring Walter Huston as a glad-handing, womanizing party hack who becomes president and is visited by the archangel Gabriel, who allows him to become sympathetic to America's unemployed. William Randolph Hearst, a Bonus Army supporter, was one of the backers of the film, which drew the ire of the notorious Hays Commission for its subversive content and had to be reedited before it was released.

By now, I've also already printed out and either skimmed or read just about every article ever printed in the *Chicago Tribune, The Washington Post, The New York Times,* and the *Los Angeles Times* that included "Bonus March," "Bonus Army," or "Bonus Expeditionary

Force"; I've used up two toner cartridges while printing articles. I've been watching Bonus Army newsreel footage on YouTube. Google alerts me every day about some new article or blog entry concerning the Bonus March, and sometimes to inform me that a hard-core band called the Bonus Army will be playing a show—I usually delete those, as I'm not particularly fond of the tunes I've found on their MySpace page.

The more I've been researching, though, the more I've started to realize how little detail my dad ever gave me about the march. My dad's contention that it represented a time when America was on the verge of a coup seems exaggerated, a story the U.S. government concocted to justify its violent actions against the veterans by unfairly characterizing their march as a dangerous Communist movement.

The story my dad told me about the Bonus March was much like the other stories he told: simple and short, but also in this case somewhat wrong. According to my dad, the marchers went to Washington; despite their valiant struggle, they left empty-handed. End of story. Or, as my brother put it in the high school paper he wrote with my dad's help, "The veterans had been denied the very rights that they had fought for in the first [*sic*] World War. Unlike in 1919, they came home defeated."

My dad never mentioned, or perhaps never knew, that the story was more complicated, that there was another bonus march in Washington, D.C., this time in 1933, during Franklin Delano Roosevelt's administration. He never told me that FDR enticed some of the campers with jobs in his Civilian Conservation Corps or that hundreds who took those jobs would die in a hurricane in Key West. He never said that FDR vetoed a bonus bill in 1935, before it actually passed in 1936. He never mentioned that the acts of the marchers may have led to the integration of the U.S. Army and the passage of the G.I. Bill. When my dad talked about the Bonus March, the impression he gave me was always that there was only one; that it began in futility, concluded in tragedy.

The marchers seem to have little connection to my dad's youth—if anything, the story my dad might have written seems like a story of someone he wasn't, a story of veterans told by a man who never served in the military; a story of the Great Depression told by someone who never spoke of his family's economic hardships during that period; a story of social movements told by a man who, to my knowledge, never took part in one; a story of wandering told by a man who, when I knew him, didn't get around much; a story of rootlessness told by a man who lived in the same home for forty-five years. The more I read, the less certain I am of why he kept talking about it.

In one of my favorite documentaries, Ross McElwee's 1986 *Sherman's March*, the filmmaker, while ostensibly tracing General Sherman's path through the South, spends most of his time and grant money trying to find girlfriends, and, in so doing, intertwines personal and American history. Though I've never made a documentary film, I've been thinking of making one about my pursuit of the connections and contradictions between my father's life and the book he wanted to write. I've made an appointment to meet McElwee in Cambridge, and on my way to our lunch, I even devise an idea for an opening series of shots—an image of my father trudging through snow on his way to work; dissolve to me walking through snow en route to the Hoover Library, where I want to conduct the research my dad never did; dissolve to black-and-white newsreel footage of Bonus Army veterans marching around the Capitol. All of us are struggling forward, persevering, seeking something we want but are unsure we'll find—truth, closure, respect. I can hear playing behind these images the last tape-recorded audio I have of my father singing the old Ink Spots song "We Three (My Echo, My Shadow, and Me)": "We three, we're are all alone."

I don't know what material I'll be able to use for a documentary, though. My dad made lots of reel-to-reel audio recordings of my family, but I've had trouble locating a cheap player so that I can listen to them. I have been watching home-movie footage of my family, but my dad didn't seem to like being on-camera. He was usually the one taking the pictures, mostly of me and my siblings when we were kids—my brother in cowboy outfits or a headdress, banging out Indian tom-toms on the metal bottom of a barrel; my sister playing piano or flinging a Wiffle ball; me helping my mother make a pizza. But when someone else took the camera and focused on my dad, he walked briskly out of the shot, shielded his face, or waved away the camera. *Stop takin' pictures of me,* he seemed to be saying. *Enough of this meshugas.* A hard man to get ahold of, hard to focus on and keep in the frame.

I meet Ross McElwee at Grafton Street, an Irish restaurant in Harvard Square, not far from his office at Harvard, where he teaches in the film department. What I like about the way McElwee makes films is that he manages to be autobiographical and self-referential without seeming self-indulgent, a tone that matches his character in person—soft-spoken, dry-witted, a hint of southern hospitality in his barely discernible drawl.

"You have to let the world come in enough so you're not totally guilty of solipsism," he advises me as we sit down for our fish and chips. "I like your idea, by the way." Though he adds that he wonders how many people know what the Bonus March is. Still, he says, "The fact that [the march] isn't well known is actually a plus, because you don't want to start with some grander way of defining your relationship with your father with a story, like 'He was a World War Two veteran.' That would be way too broad."

I've been thinking about how to incorporate all the books and articles I've been gathering with the story of my dad, how to blend the historical with the personal, which right now seem to be at odds. I point out that *Sherman's March* seems to have very little information about the march from which it takes its title.

"You just have to lift a tiny percentage of what you're reading," McElwee says. "I did this with my film. I read six or seven books that were voluminous in detail about his march and about Sherman as a person. I read two entire biographies of Sherman, way more material than I could ever use, but I took a lot of notes and ended up using maybe one-point-zero-zero percent of what I read. I'm driven by curiosity. It wasn't a chore for me to read all of those books. And it was useful to me as I was tracing his route through the South. I would meet someone at a historical site and I would be able to say something about what happened there because I had read a certain book about that particular moment in history."

"Were you aware at the time that you were going to use so little of what you were reading?" I ask.

"I knew that I wanted to work in the present tense," McElwee says, "but I was very much flying by the seat of my pants. I never do wholesale historical explorations. There's nothing wrong with it, but that's not what I do. With my kind of filmmaking and the kind of work you're doing, it's impossible to know the structure in advance."

"Were you always very conscious that you would be that sort of artist?" I ask.

"For me, it was just a more interesting way to live," says McElwee. "I always knew that I was much more interested in going into the world with a camera on my shoulder, responding to things that were happening at that moment, and shooting ten times more footage than I needed, then getting back to the editing room, trying to shape a story out of all this raw material, and that's what you'll probably be doing—gathering, taking lots of notes on things that may not be of any use to you. When I start working on a project, it's just propelled by my own intuition and curiosity and sense that there is a good story, and I'm not even sure if that story is right, but I'll find out as I go along."

We spend lunch discussing my project, the interviews I'm beginning to set up with people who knew my father, the trips I'm planning to locations relevant to the Bonus March. Then McElwee asks, "What, for you, is the central mystery about your father?"

And for me right now, the answer is the Bonus March. Not the historical incident specifically. Not even necessarily the fact that my dad wanted to write about it or that he ultimately didn't. The mystery is what that event represents for me—a key to my dad's inner life, to closing the distance I felt when I was with him, to learning what shaped him, to understanding what may have been going on in his mind, to understanding my own detachment from him, too. My father never told me his dreams, and the Bonus March book is the closest thing to a dream I know. The more I learn about it, the closer I may get to understanding my dad.

I ask McElwee if he thinks my journey might make for a good film.

"Well," he says, "I'm trying to get a sense of how much of this would present material that could be filmed, as opposed to researched and written, which is the writer's way of dealing with the past. Unless you have some remarkably provocative home-movie footage or some really special still photographs that seem like more than what that generic material usually is, I think it is probably a project that you'd be better off writing as a book."

1975

I'm eight years old and I have a very idyllic image of my parents' childhoods on the old West Side of Chicago. Most of my friends listen to Top 40 music on WLS and WCFL, but my three favorite radio shows are "Music from Broadway," "The Hall Closet," and "Those Were the Days." Those last two are hosted by Chuck Schaden, who is Chicago's authority on old-time radio. Schaden plays such programs as "Suspense," "The Shadow," and "The Jack

Benny Show," all of which were popular when my parents were growing up. I listen as much as I can to these shows every weekday morning and every Saturday afternoon. Sometimes at home, I use a portable tape recorder to make my own radio plays.

Since I have never seen my parents' neighborhood or talked with them about their past in any great detail, I maintain a romantic image of my folks as kids gathered with their families around the radio. I'm particularly fond of listening to stories dramatized by Orson Welles's Mercury Theatre on the Air, and I'm fascinated by how, in October 1938, Welles fooled America into thinking it was being invaded by Martians during his adaptation of H. G. Wells's *War of the Worlds*.

This afternoon, my dad's driving me back from my piano lesson at Mrs. Schwartzberg's, and my mom's in the front seat. We're listening to an episode of "Fibber McGee and Molly," a comedy program that was the country's top-rated show when my parents were kids. It doesn't seem all that funny to me, but I assume my parents are enjoying it. During a commercial break ("Heeey, don't touch that dial; we'll be right back"), I ask my mother about "War of the Worlds"— had she and my father felt scared when it was broadcast?

No, my mother says. She knew Orson Welles's voice—everybody did—and anyone who thought we were being invaded by Martians must have been some kind of moron.

And what about "Fibber McGee and Molly"? I ask my father. Did he sit with his family and listen to that show whenever it came on?

No, that show was terrible, my father tells me—whenever it came on the radio, he turned it off.

WASHINGTON, D.C.

I

At the corner of Third Street and Pennsylvania Avenue, I sit on a concrete bench by a bronze statue of eighteenth-century legal scholar William Blackstone and look toward the National Gallery of Art. To my left is the U.S. Capitol, white and resplendent on this cloudless blue-sky day. A few blocks up is the Newseum, a 25,000-square-foot museum dedicated to the pursuit of journalism. Here on Pennsylvania Avenue, in some way, is the condensed story of the Bonus March, its legacy, and my relationship to it, too.

Back in the summer of 1932, the future site of the National Gallery was a forest, from which campers would gather firewood. Bonus camps were located on the site of the Newseum. Farther up Pennsylvania Avenue is the White House, where Herbert Hoover issued his July 28 order that would seal the fate of the Bonus Marchers, and his own as well. "Surround the affected area and clear it without delay," Secretary of War Patrick Hurley ordered General MacArthur.

Veterans had been ordered to evacuate government-owned buildings, including a half-demolished three-story redbrick car dealership on Pennsylvania and Third. The street corner where I am sitting marks where officers of the Treasury Department, assisted by the D.C. police, began evacuating the men.

In the early afternoon, the building that was here was just about cleared when fights broke out between police and veterans, many of whom were converging on this avenue from other nearby encampments. As police advanced with nightsticks, a cry of "Let's get him" erupted from the vets. Bricks were hurled at police officers, one of whom drew a gun and fired. "For God's sake, stop that shooting!" Police Chief Pelham Glassford shouted, but the warning came too late. Bonus Army member William Hushka, an out-of-work Lithuanian butcher and Great War veteran who had been recruited for the Bonus March off a bread line in Chicago, was dead, and another marcher, Eric Carlson, had been mortally wounded. A third veteran, John Hall, had been shot in the stomach, and policeman George Scott was headed for the hospital with a fractured skull. By late afternoon, cavalry troops were on their way.

Today, helmeted tourists on Segway personal transporters speed up and down the sidewalk where just over seventy-five years ago onlookers gathered to watch soldiers riding on horseback or marching in file, bayonets drawn. Some of the vets and the other spectators applauded the soldiers until they realized what they were doing here. The soldiers donned gas masks as they lobbed tear-gas canisters that sent the marchers fleeing from demolished buildings, shacks, and tents, thousands of which were burned to the ground. "It was a bad-looking mob which we faced on Pennsylvania Avenue, and it was animated by the essence of revolution," General MacArthur would say.

None of this history is visible now; campgrounds and shanty-towns have long since been replaced by museums, by government buildings, by the butterfly garden of the Museum of Natural History. Seventy-five years ago, Washington was in a state of chaos during a time of peace; today, in a time of war, all is peaceful. During the week I've been staying in Washington, I've spotted only five people protesting anything—three abortion opponents in front of the Supreme Court Building, standing with the word *LIFE* printed on black tape stuck over their mouths; near the gates of the White House, a pair of women protesting nuclear weapons. Occasionally, I have seen soldiers in uniform, but they're nowhere near as prevalent as lobbyists, easily identifiable by their company badges.

Earlier today, on the Ellipse, which in 1932 served as Douglas MacArthur's staging grounds, I watched government workers smooth out a long, narrow path of dirt on the otherwise-green lawn; tourists fed nuts to squirrels, then photographed them. In the Newseum, there was only one sign of the marchers' history, even though much action actually played out where the museum stands. On the sixth floor, in a gallery of newspaper front pages, a two-paragraph story from a 1932 issue of the Camden *Courier-Post* was headlined FULL CASH PAYMENT URGED FOR VETS. But the biggest story in the Camden paper was the tragic saga of the Lindbergh baby; the plight of the Bonus veterans received a treatment no bigger than a baseball box score.

Evalyn Walsh McLean, a fixture of early-twentieth-century D.C. society, owner of the Hope diamond, author of *Father Struck It Rich*, and one of the benefactors of the Bonus March, a woman who helped provide for Bonus Army commander W. W. Waters's lodgings and once purchased one thousand sandwiches at Childs' Restaurant and donated them to the veterans, used to live in a Beaux-Arts mansion on Massachusetts Avenue. The building remains intact, along with its yellow skylight, chandeliers, and stained-glass windows, all by Tiffany, but today the home serves as the Indonesian embassy. The Hope diamond is in the Museum of Natural History.

On the National Mall, that long, verdant passage between the Capitol and the Washington Monument, famous as a site of protests and rallies, information kiosks and gift booths can be found where in 1932 camps were occupied by the left-wing contingent of the Bonus Army.

On the bronze statue's pedestal here at Pennsylvania and Third, the name *Blackstone* is tough to make out at first; the letters have been worn down. At a glance, the figure resembles some anonymous jurist; he could be any man at all. With the judicial wig, he could even be the actor Bert Lahr playing the Cowardly Lion in *The Wizard of Oz*. But to me, he more closely resembles my father—the thoughtful, imperturbable facial expression, cognizant that he knows something I don't, the wise eyes never quite meeting mine. Not a mean expression, really, just occupied with matters of greater importance than my presence. *What are you doin' here? Just cockin' around?*

the statue seems to ask me. *Are you on your way in or on your way out? You expect to make a livin' from this? Didja ever get around to takin' those LSATs?*

I walk around the statue to see if I can catch his glance, but no, he keeps looking beyond—to the sites where the U.S. Army and the Bonus Army did battle, toward the Capitol, which on that day in late July would have been shrouded in smoke from tear gas and the flames that erupted when the campers' tents were set ablaze. One of Blackstone's bronze hands clutches a book. There's no title on it, so it really could be any book, and as I stand beneath the statue, I imagine that the book has no title because it was one that was never written about an event that happened here but has left no discernible trace, an event that the statue's eyes continue to watch, an event that I am continuing to seek and understand, even though all physical signs of it seem to have disappeared.

II

My father talked to me about wanting to interview surviving members of the Bonus Army for his book; he wrote his letters to *The New York Times Book Review*, requesting eyewitness reports. But today, any actual marcher would have to be well over one hundred years old. And even the youngest people who witnessed the event are in their late seventies.

Naaman Seigle is seated at the bar of the National Press Club. Born in 1925, the same year as my dad, Seigle was once a regional newspaper reporter, and he worked as an economist for the U.S. Department of Agriculture. A soft-spoken, owlish man, he wears a thick red flannel shirt and thicker glasses. Anytime I want to find him, he says, I should come to the Press Club; he has few other places to go anymore. Like the marchers my dad wanted to commemorate, he, too, is now part of a disappearing generation.

"I've got nothing else to do," Seigle says. "I'm here five days a week, maybe six. I'm losing my sight. I have macular degeneration due to arterial sclerosis, and I don't read the paper; I only scan it. I've got nothing to do, not a damn thing on television."

Seigle was seven during the Bonus March. He was the son of a pharmacist who ran one of the few apothecary shops in the southwest of the city. He was too young to know about the details of the march, but when he would walk through the city with his father, he could see the Eleventh Street Bridge and the Navy Yard. He remembers watching veterans cross the bridge into the city to march and mill about the Capitol, then take the same bridge back to their camps. When MacArthur and his men came to disperse the Bonus Army, that bridge was the one the veterans had to take out of town on their way toward Johnstown, Pennsylvania, where that town's pugnacious mayor, Eddie McCloskey, had promised to provide shelter for them.

On July 28, 1932, Seigle had gone with his dad to buy a new table radio for their home. They already had a big Philco and wanted a smaller one. Seigle and his dad were walking on 4 1/2 Street, heading back home to 452 M Street with their new radio, when they saw the troops.

"And then what?" I ask.

"I got tear-gassed," he says.

"I imagine you were terrified."

" 'Terrified' wasn't the word for it."

Confused, scared, and in pain, Seigle ran home with his father; his mother made him take a bath to wash out his eyes.

"I was crying like hell," Seigle says now.

"Was your dad hurt, too?"

"Yeah, but at least he knew what was going on. I sure as hell didn't.

"I was just so scared," he says. "Maybe I had nightmares—I don't remember that. I just know I was scared. But when we were at home, I remember I looked out the window on M Street and watched the cavalry march from Fort Myer up over to the Navy Yard. After it was all over, we went down to the Anacostia Flats, where camps used to be, and we saw all the burned-out buildings. I can still picture them today, seventy-five years later."

"Did the radio survive?"

"Oh yes," Seigle says. "My dad was pretty proud of that; my mother was, too. After we had gone through all that, we still had two radios."

"Will you be here tomorrow?" I ask.

"It depends on the weather," says Seigle. "If it's warm enough for me to walk, I'll be here."

III

The Historical Society of Washington, D.C., houses the city's most extensive archives concerning the Bonus March—fourteen containers of books and documents, most donated by historians Tom Allen and Paul Dickson, authors of *The Bonus Army: An American Epic.* But the librarian here tells me I'm the first person who has requested to look at anything in the archives; in one hall adjacent to the reading room, there is an exhibit of photographs and artifacts of the Bonus March. While the librarian checks in back to look for files I've requested, I investigate the exhibit room.

Inside a glass case are a tear-gas gun, a nightstick, and a police officer's badge; on a wall are lyrics to "Brother, Can You Spare a Dime?" the song that has been said to have been inspired in part by the plight of the Bonus March veterans. There are framed pages from the Bonus Army's official newspaper, the *B.E.F. News,* photographs of Camp Glassford, named after the D.C. police chief, of men bathing in the Anacostia River, of a child holding a sign that reads I'M HELPING MY DADDY GET THE BONUS, of Bonus Army commander Walter W. Waters in riding boots and jodhpurs, of Douglas MacArthur in military dress. But I'm the only person in this room.

Three dozen chairs are arranged in front of a low podium, but no one sits in the chairs and no one is speaking before them.

In the reading room, I pore over the *B.E.F. News,* a complete set of the newspapers that were published starting on June 25, 1932, right in the middle of the veterans' stay in Washington, D.C., and ending in October of the same year, after they'd been forced out of both the capital and Johnstown, Pennsylvania. I scan headlines, trying to find some connection to my dad or one of his relatives, but with no success. Most of what catches my eye are marginal stories, tragic human-interest tales populated by long-forgotten men and women: ARMY NURSE SUFFERS BREAKDOWN AT CAMP; DESTITUTE MOTHER SEARCHES FOR LOST SON; NEED OF MILK FOR BABIES OF B.E.F. STIRS VETERANS.

The *B.E.F. News* is such an obscure and rare paper that I entertain myself with the idea of inserting a fake article into my notes that would help to make a direct connection between my family and the Bonus March: "Young Soda Jobber Asserts His Support for the Bonus—Great War Vet Sam Langer, Seen Here in the Company of His Eldest Son, Seymour Sidney, Bivouacs at Camp Marks" or "7-Year-Old Langer, Citing Experience of His Father, Writes Letter Denouncing Treatment of Vets." When I was in school, I used to make up lots of stories—my maternal grandmother's maiden name was Shor, so I would say that I was related to Dinah Shore. But I'm not in school anymore, and I'm not writing a novel, either. I'm trying to tell my father's story as faithfully as I can, and the truth is that nothing in these archives allows me to make any real connection between the Bonus March and my dad.

IV

In 2004, when my father and I were still discussing the Bonus March project, the book most like the one my dad wanted to write was published. *The Bonus Army: An American Epic* is a comprehensive history of the march. It examines the march's origins, its impact, and the reason for its obscurity, which authors Tom Allen and Paul Dickson blame on the controversial racial integration of the movement well in advance of the integration of the army, the negative light in which the events placed not only Herbert Hoover but also Franklin Delano Roosevelt and Douglas MacArthur, and the successful public-relations effort that characterized the march as a primarily radical movement.

Tom Allen is from my father's generation, born in 1929, and he, too, is a fan of Barbara Tuchman. He's an old-school journalist, and he looks the part—ruddy complexion, salt-and-pepper brush mustache, the sardonic, world-weary humor of a onetime beat reporter. He worked as a Sunday features writer for the New York *Daily News,* and as an editor and writer for *National Geographic.* Today, I'm sitting in the passenger seat of his car and we're driving around D.C., looking for anything that remains of the Bonus March.

"So," Allen asks me, "do you know anything about your father's experience in the camps here? What state did he come out of? They divided everything into states. Would he have been Illinois?"

"No," I say. "My father actually wasn't in the march, as far as I know. He was interested because his dad was a veteran."

As Allen steers and points out sites, I try to imagine the city with all the new buildings erased, all the tourists replaced by men in white shirts and straw hats, carrying signs and marching toward the Capitol. I try to imagine the cloudless sky, full of tear gas and smoke; I try to imagine flames shooting up, blocking out the Capitol dome.

None of it's still here. Even the bridge that led the marchers from the Capitol to Anacostia is gone, Allen tells me. Near where that bridge used to be is the baseball stadium for the Washington Nationals. In 1932, the local major-league team was the Senators, managed by Walter Johnson and featuring Moe Berg, Joe Cronin, and Heinie Manush. They played at Griffith Stadium, where boxing matches were held to benefit the vets of the Bonus Army. At

Anacostia, there once was a proposal to commemorate the Bonus March with a memorial, but it doesn't exist now and probably never did.

"It was going to be a flagpole at the main encampment," Allen says, "but we could never find a record of it. Whether it was ever erected or not isn't clear. The authorities in one of the military airports said it would be a hazard to flights, which was bullshit. At the very beginning of our research, we got a lot of cooperation from the Historical Society and they gave us lots of access to material, but we never found out anything about that flagpole. We tried to get the Park Service interested in doing something about it, but they worry about things like the Lincoln Memorial and the Washington Monument; they don't worry about what happened across the street. And as far as veterans' groups are concerned, there's almost an abhorrence of the whole event."

We take the highway to Anacostia, where we drive along Good Hope Road. It's Park Service land over here—government offices, a helicopter, an empty building. Inside an office building, we ask one of the historians working here if he knows anything about the march, what used to be where. He says no.

"Has anyone ever come in here asking about it?" I ask. "There was a time when thousands of people were camping right here."

"Not that I can recall."

"Nobody knows anything," Tom Allen says as we leave, then jokes, "If you want to kill somebody, do it on park property; it'll never be solved."

"Every country has a grand story," Allen tells me as we have coffee in the National Gallery of Art. He then cites a theory he attributes to Barbara Tuchman to explain why the Bonus March has been so overlooked: "There was a grand story of the Depression: 'Brother, Can You Spare a Dime?,' selling apples on the corner, the dust storms, *The Grapes of Wrath,* blah, blah, blah. Everything bad was done by Hoover. FDR comes and saves the day and the Depression ends. Well, in that grand story, FDR is supposed to help the veterans, and he doesn't. And he's supposed to be championing all these forgotten people, and he really doesn't. The Bonus Army doesn't fit in with the grand story. And I think that's one of the reasons why it hasn't been told.

"It's really a twisted story. I loved Roosevelt. He was a saint in my house when I was growing up. I was shocked that Roosevelt turned out to be antiveteran, and his 'little guy and forgotten man' routine didn't extend to the Bonus Marchers. That story doesn't fit in with the grand story."

Allen asks why my father wanted to write the book. I say that I believe he wanted to honor the memories of his father's generation and his father's service but that I'm not yet sure why that was so important to him. Allen asks why I'm doing this research, and I say that I want to make sure the stories my father wanted to tell aren't forgotten, either, that I want to preserve the dreams of his generation, just as he wanted to preserve his father's. And as I speak to Allen, I wonder if I'm at all right in understanding my father's motives. And I wonder, too, about my father's "grand story"—what parts did he leave out?

V

On the way out of D.C., I take the Metro to Arlington Cemetery to visit the grave of William Hushka, the Lithuanian immigrant from Chicago who served as a private during World War I and was the first of two marchers to die for their cause. His funeral was attended by a guard of honor composed of two members of the Bonus Army, two members each from various American Legion and VFW posts, and a detail of troops from Fort Myer. His body was carried on a caisson past the White House.

Hushka's grave is located at the outermost reaches of the cemetery, nearly a half-hour walk from Arlington's main entrance. To get there, I walk along Eisenhower Drive, which seems somehow appropriate. The stories of men such as Eisenhower who helped drive out the marchers are still told; the stories of the routed veterans are the ones that have been forgotten.

Arlington is, of course, the final resting place for presidents, Supreme Court justices, and war heroes, but the thousands of forgotten names on these other gravestones, all lined up like marble dominoes, pearl white against carpets of green, have greater resonance for me. In brilliant sunshine, I walk along Eisenhower Drive to a road lined by oaks and pine trees, and I consider the thousands of missing stories here, the lost stories, forgotten stories, buried stories, the ones that may never be told. Those of William Hushka and the Bonus Army, of Seymour Sidney Langer and his unwritten book, and of these names on headstones:

Terrill, Lutz, Calhoun.

At one grave site, two little girls, one in pink, one in green, are placing roses by a grave.

Smiley, Schell, Becker.

Three military men in their dress blacks sit by another grave, passing back and forth a bottle of liquor in a paper bag.

Rawls, Terrell, Hampson.

Two ebony horses are pulling a cart; upon it is a metal casket draped in black.

William Hushka's grave is located in section 18 of the cemetery. His is a simple marble headstone: "William J. Hushka, PFC, 41 INF, 10 DIV." No birth date, just the date of his death—July 28, 1932. Overhead, a crow caws. Locusts buzz. An airplane soars. As I look at the headstone and the other surrounding graves, I can hear a bagpiper playing.

The takeoff from Washington National Airport is fast. Unlike a view I had out of an airplane approaching Chicago, when I could stare out the window for minutes at just about every place my father had ever been, here, the images pass in an instant. Somewhere down there below the clouds is a bronze statue of a man who resembles my dad, clutching a nameless book and gazing out at the street and at the story of the Bonus March.

My Father's Generation: Scene from a Documentary

PART I: THE OLD NEIGHBORHOOD

There are still many men and women alive who walked the same streets that my father walked, grew up during the same Great Depression he did, lived out stories comparable to his. They, too, were the sons and daughters of immigrants who, at the beginning of the twentieth century, left Eastern Europe with barely a shekel, packed into ships that journeyed to Ellis Island, found their way to Chicago and the city's West Side. They lived in my father's neighborhood during the time of the Bonus March, witnessed the days of my dad's youth, knew the boy he was before he became the man I knew. I've begun seeking out the stories of these men and women, listening to their voices, asking them what they remember about the Bonus March, what it meant to them and what it might have meant to him, and I'm beginning to feel like Thompson, the reporter in Citizen Kane *who asks everyone he meets the same question and usually receives the same unsatisfying answers. "Did he ever happen to say anything about Rosebud? . . . You're not Rosebud, are you?" Did you ever hear him say anything about the Bonus March?*

VOICES: **Howard Watt,** my father's classmate at Penn Elementary School and Marshall High; **Seymour Levine,** my father's classmate at Marshall High and the University of Illinois; **Jerome Langer,** my father's brother; **Norm Budow,** my father's grade school and high school classmate and next-door neighbor; **Mitchell Schorow,** my father's high school and college classmate; **Lenny Primer,** my father's best friend; **Jerry Singer,** my father's cousin; **Sheldon Schoneberg,** my father's high school and medical school classmate; **Millicent Marks,** my father's high school classmate; **Pepi Singer,** my father's cousin.

HOWARD WATT

"GVS" is what we called it. The Great *Vest Side.*

SEYMOUR LEVINE

Oh, the West Side of Chicago in the thirties was a real phenomenon when we were growing up. On the Jewish holidays, you couldn't see the streets because they were so crowded with Jews. That's how thick it was on Rosh Hashanah. You'd walk down Independence Boulevard and all you saw was people out in front of the steps of the synagogues. Along Independence, there were a dozen different synagogues. Every couple of blocks there was a synagogue, and every one was crowded. Things came to a halt on the Jewish holidays.

JEROME LANGER

The apartment buildings were mostly Jewish. There was only one Jew in the neighborhood who had a house. All the rest lived in apartments. The houses, the bungalows, were all Italian and Irish.

NORM BUDOW

We lived in a four-room apartment in a three-flat; there were two apartments on each floor. A shoemaker named Pusateri had a shop down below and he made toys for the neighborhood kids around Christmas. One of the girls who lived in our building was named Laraine Beatus, and she had a sister Geraldine, who was going with an usher at the Crawford Movie House, and he would let us in for free if the boss wasn't around. We lived with my aunt and uncle, who were labor Zionists. I have childhood memories of them singing songs, playing instruments, talking about returning to the ancient homeland, where there would be a new kind of Jew who would work the land. Your dad's family lived across the hall from us.

MITCHELL SCHOROW

My dad was a shoe man. He started out in Russia as an apprentice leather maker, and then he came to Downers Grove, Illinois. It was a small farming town of three or four thousand, with barely any Jews in it, only two or three Jewish families, a weird place. Once, the Silver Shirts, a neo-Nazi organization, paraded down the main street. My dad always told us we were like guests of the town. One time I had a fight with a kid and his dad called my father, and when I came home, my dad gave me a licking. He said, "You're not supposed to fight." When we came to Chicago, I was scared to death. All we knew about Chicago was gangsters and Al Capone. The West Side turned out to be a hell of a lot better than Downers Grove.

HOWARD WATT

We had a restaurant called Watt's on Sixteenth and Lawndale. It started out in about 1932 or '33. When I was six years old, I would come home from school and take care of the candy department. You could get about five or six candies there for a penny.

LENNY PRIMER

My father was a barber. He and his brother had a shop on Roosevelt Road. They came over from Europe by themselves when my dad was twelve years old. My dad didn't have any experience being a barber, but everybody had to do something and someone had to do that work, so they gave him a scissors.

JERRY SINGER

For all the years we knew your dad's father, he was always "the pop man." He worked hard, everybody did, but he was the hardest-working guy you ever wanted to run into. He schlepped those big bottles and he was always on the run—fast, fast, fast.

NORM BUDOW

One of the things your grandfather delivered was seltzer in the bottles you *shpritz;* they don't even have those anymore.

HOWARD WATT

The Bonus March? Sure, I remember it well. I remember the money my mother got—it was after my father died. Oh, I remember it very well. I remember there were songs about it. I remember the Depression very well. A lot of sharing went on in the Depression. Back then, my grandfather, as a butcher, fed I don't know how many people. My mother knew some people in the neighborhood who had literally nothing to eat to speak of, and once a week she would make a huge pot of soup with meat in it, and my chore was to deliver it. But people were very proud, so I couldn't walk through the street and go to the front door; I had to go through the alley and get up the back steps to deliver this stuff so that people wouldn't see what I was doing.

LENNY PRIMER

I met your dad on the first day of high school. We both walked into Miss Mertz's German class. I'd never met him before; he was on crutches at that time. You want to hear something crazy? I was without a doubt your father's closest friend, and I never once asked him, "What's wrong with your legs?" Not once.

HOWARD WATT

I met him at Penn Elementary School. He was short and stocky, very strong up top, and he had these terrible legs. He walked in a weird fashion, threw himself one way or the other, very hard for him to walk and keep his balance. Some of the kids would pick on Sy, push him, say all kinds of nasty things, try to knock him over. That was the way of being cruel and stupid back then. But I would stand with him, and they went away. Nobody fussed with him when I stood with him.

SHELDON SCHONEBERG

I never found out what was wrong with his hips. It was never discussed. He would always keep up with us, but I know darn well it was a struggle for him.

HOWARD WATT

Don't forget he was self-educated, so to speak, because of all that time he spent in the hospital. But when he got to school, he immediately picked up and got into the right age group. Brilliant kid, absolutely.

MILLICENT MARKS

He was always very goal-oriented. He stuck to his science and math projects. He was definitely going into medicine. He was always experimenting. His hands were big, but he could cut up and dissect the most intricate little insect and get every part without a flaw.

SHELDON SCHONEBERG

The biggest influence that your father and I had was a teacher named Enid Hennessy. She was a little lady about five feet tall, a real stickler. She made you learn your science, your anatomy, the different classifications of animals, birds, plants, flowers. She was the reason we were going to be doctors.

MILLICENT MARKS

She was a real character, a very exciting little woman, very small, very wiry. When I was trying to get answers from your father, she would call out, "Hey, you!" And I would turn and say, "What what what what

what?" And she'd say, "Get out of his face!" And I'd say, "I just want one answer, let me get just one!"

Norm Budow
Her nickname was "Scratchball" Hennessy. She gave me a pain in my lower regions.

Howard Watt
She had two sets of questions—one had eight hundred questions; the other had thirteen hundred questions. In order to answer them, you had to go to the Field Museum. We would head up there Saturday during the day; then we'd go on State Street, eat lunch, and pal around together.

Seymour Levine
Everyone looked up to your dad. He was on a higher plane of intelligence or something. I remember your dad running, absolutely running down the corridors of Marshall High School, and as I picture him in my mind, he is carrying a briefcase in his hand and waving as he goes by.

Mitchell Schorow
Seymour was the smartest of our bunch. Whatever he knew, he knew, and whatever he didn't know, he didn't know. He would never say he knew something when he didn't know it, and you could count on him for being straightforward, practical.

Pepi Singer
He was what you call a mensch. You know what a mensch is? A true person.

Sheldon Schoneberg
But the Bonus March? Yeah, World War One veterans, right, that's where they came in and destroyed the tent city. I remember that. But I

have no real knowledge of that. I don't recall your father ever expressing a desire to write. None of us became writers.

CHICAGO

I

Near the end of May 1932, when the Bonus March began, my dad was in first grade at Penn Elementary School; the country's unemployment rate was nearly 25 percent. In Cook County, foreclosures had reached an all-time high. At Chicago's Majestic Theatre, jobless actors staged a benefit show called *Breadline Frolics.* On Twenty-third and Michigan, near where my grandfather Sam Langer had worked as a bartender, the Immanuel Baptist Church was shutting down its breadlines because it didn't have enough money. And at the railyards at Cottage Grove and East Seventy-fifth Street, five hundred veterans were hopping freight cars to join the others, who were either already in or on their way to Washington, D.C., to ask for their "bonus."

In Chicago, Bonus veterans raised money in Grant Park for their trip and subsisted on food and beverages provided by local businesses and the American Legion. Railroad companies donated empty train cars to take the veterans over the Indiana border.

I continue to be inundated with material about the Bonus Army. Finding information about my dad in order to discover the connection between him and the history he wanted to write has been tougher. The only articles I've tracked down about my father during his youth offer little to contradict the image I already have of a brainy, driven, and somewhat smart-ass kid—one article from a January 1943 edition of the *Chicago Daily Tribune* names him one of the city's top high school seniors, and lists his credentials: member of the Junior Red Cross, president of the student council, school representative on the "Citizens of Tomorrow" radio show. Another *Tribune* article from the same month reveals both that he won a one-hundred-dollar scholarship to attend the University of Illinois and that the dry and somewhat macabre sensibility I would get to know twenty-five years later was already in full effect: "His hobby is dissecting animals, such as rats, in order to study them," the article's author asserts.

Today, it's a warm, sunny spring day and I've driven from my mother's house to Waldheim Cemetery in search of the graves of my father's parents. Here, most of my father's side of the family, though not my father, is buried. Waldheim, when I was growing up, was a word that was rarely spoken but whose significance seemed immense whenever it was. Like Dunning, the hospital for the mentally ill. Or the Audy Home, where juvenile delinquents were sent: "Watch out for that kid; he came from the *Audy Home*." "You heard what happened to him? They locked him up in *Dunning*." "Well, nothin's gonna help him; he's in *Waldheim* now."

As a child, I was shielded from most all events involving death or funerals, so I never came here. I remember sitting in the audience of the Goodman Theatre with my mom and dad and hearing it discussed in a one-act play by David Mamet, *The Disappearance of the Jews*:

Bobby: You been out to Waldheim?
Joey: Judy and I went last month. We try to go once a month.

I remember thinking, Once a month? I've never been there at all.

Founded in 1873, Waldheim, where more than 150,000 Jews are buried, is a quick trip from the Eisenhower Expressway. It stands in the shadow of Wal-Mart and Kmart, and it's divided into lots: one for Ezras Israel's congregation, one for this synagogue's congregation, one for that synagogue's. In the small, bleak office, a heavyset bearded man seated behind a desk asks for my grandparents' names, then types them into his database. KC and the Sunshine Band are singing on the office boom box: "Shake Your Booty." The man gives me a map and directions.

My grandparents' graves are hard to find, but once I reach the intersection of Abraham and Rebecca streets, I see I've gone too far. Not much of a crowd here today. The atmosphere seems peaceful, and yet the solemnity is somewhat disturbed by the fact that I can see a low, windowless warehouse to the immediate south and, just to the north, Gleason Chevrolet and Portillo's Hot Dogs. I steer my rental car into the P.O.W. section of the cemetery, then get out and stroll. I wonder if P.O.W. refers to time my grandfather spent in a prisoner-of-war camp during World War I, but none of the gravestones I pass offer any information about military service.

The cemetery feels ancient, European, labyrinthine. Overgrown grass obscures graves that do not receive perpetual care. The graves seem not so much neglected as long past their primes. On the grave of someone who died young, these words are inscribed: "I had no regrets upon leaving for I knew not why I was here." The image of the man to whom these sentiments have been attributed has been worn away.

The grass crunches as I step on it. I look down—cicada shells. Something is beginning to emerge, something that's been buried for years, an autobiography inscribed in the lives of cicadas. Seventeen years have passed since the last time this brood of cicadas was in Chicago, and now that I look more closely, I see them everywhere. The first time I saw them, I was in the backseat of one of my father's black Fords, riding back from a picnic in the woods; my brother was in the front seat, blasting Argent's "Hold Your Head Up" on the radio. The cicadas all but covered the windshield. The second time I saw cicadas, I was already an adult, a journalist working on a story in Highland Park, Illinois, and I remember cicadas hovering over me as

I emerged from my car. Today, I am a father and my father is gone, and there they are, crawling out of their shells, lying atop headstones and monuments, on my grandfather's gravestone: "Died July 2, 1974."

Samuel Langer's is the smallest and the newest gravestone in the plot. Cicadas crawl upon it. Cicada shells are on the gravestones of ancestors whose names I vaguely recognize. The cicadas cover the monument to my grandmother Rebecca Langer. Cicadas crawl over the image of Eva Popko, my grandmother's mother, who died in 1916. They are emerging from their shells, hovering over my grand-father's grave.

But no more information is here. Just dates and memories. "No money to be made here," my father liked to say. Nothing about the rank Sam Langer may have had in the military or where he may have fought. P.O.W., as it turns out, stands for Progressive Order of the West, a fraternal organization founded in the early 1900s by Jewish immigrants from Poland and Russia, and has nothing to do with the U.S. armed forces.

At the end of the day, I write a letter to the National Personnel Records Center in St. Louis, inquiring about what exactly my grand-father did during World War I.

II

Continuing to search for remnants of the life my father had before I knew him, I drive along the streets of the old West Side, occasionally glancing down at addresses I have scrawled on envelopes: 4161 Fifth Avenue, where my dad lived with his family when he was a kid; 1851 S. Harding Street, where my dad's maternal aunt Bessie Cohen lived with her three children.

Neither building is there. Instead, there are empty lots with over-grown weeds. FOR SALE signs are stuck in the ground in the middle of this blighted neighborhood, the likes of which I haven't seen since the 1970s. Men loiter on street corners, on fire escapes; they drink out of paper bags. Near the empty lot at my dad's corner at Keeler and Fifth, smoke billows from a barbecue. When I stop the car, a guy on the corner with a cell phone shouts "Yo!" across the street to his buddy, who is also speaking into a cell phone. The buddy puts down his phone, gets a look at me, apparently decides I'm not a dealer, a buyer, or a cop, and returns to his phone conversation. I want to knock on a door, tell someone my dad used to live here, but I sense that no one would give a damn. I keep driving, listening to the voices of my father and my relatives warning me: *Why would you wanna go back? You could get yourself killed.*

On the 700 block of South Laflin Street, there are rehabbed buildings in the now-gentrifying Italian neighborhood where my grandfather lived after he arrived from Europe. At 1626 S. Spring-field, where my dad's family lived for a time, there's another empty lot and a windowless brick building where perhaps a factory once operated. At 1815 S. Avers, site of another one of my dad's family's apartments, is a rectangle of dead grass, a realty company's sign in the ground. The pop factory, S & L Beverages, is a fenced-in yard— trash strewn upon dead or overgrown grass. A housing project looms in the distance. My father's youth in Chicago seems as invisible as the Bonus March in Washington.

III

I'm on the old West Side, walking along Douglas Boulevard with my friend Paula Kamen. She is speaking loudly into her cell phone. "Is that the place you were talking about across the street from the JPI?" she asks. "Some kind of theological seminary? No?"

"Paula?" I ask.

Paula is the author of four nonfiction books—*Feminist Fatale, Her Way, All in My Head,* and *Finding Iris Chang.* She went to col-lege downstate with my oldest friend, Paul Creamer, where both worked for the *Daily Illini*, just like my dad's pal Gene Shalit did forty years earlier. Paula and I met about fifteen years ago, when I was editing a fledgling arts and culture magazine and I assigned her a story about the indie movie *Go Fish*, paying her out of my own pocket when the magazine couldn't afford the fifty bucks we owed her. Paula is one of the smartest and funniest people I know, and she has a certain blithe obliviousness that is charming in nearly all situations—nearly all.

"What's the address, Dad? 704 Homan?"

"Uh, Paula?" I ask.

Tonight, we're walking away from the arched doorway of what was once the Jewish People's Institute. The JPI, a community center where my father used to meet with his high school buddies, is now the Lawndale Community Academy, a public school, which tonight hosted a performance of Jewish and African American sacred music, attempting to find affinities between cantors and gospel singers, a connection between the neighborhood's present and its past. But the connection seems tenuous. This was once the hub of Jewish youth activity in Chicago; today, the building is deteriorating and the neighborhood around it feels desolate. Part of tonight's show was scuttled when the boom box onstage, the one element of modern technology, broke. Many wooden seats in the auditorium were broken, too. One thing is the same as it was in the 1930s, though—no air conditioning.

"Homan between Harrison and Flournoy?" Paula shouts into her cell phone, glances down at a piece of paper with some scribbles on it, then says to nobody in particular, "I can't read my own handwriting."

Paula is talking on the phone with her dad, Joseph Kamen, a graduate of Marshall High School. Paula's grandfather was a butcher on the West Side and her father is now an industrial psychologist. Her uncle Jack was in my dad's graduating class at Marshall, and Paula and I are trying to find where her family used to live and work.

As we walk away from the old JPI building, we are treading the paths of our ancestors, about whom neither of us ever learned much; we're Generation X children of Depression-era folks who left the West Side decades before we were conscious.

"Dad, Dad, wait a minute, what?" Paula says.

Over Paula's shoulder is an open bag, from which she's extracted pen and paper to write down addresses, and I'm getting nervous— no matter how much time I've spent in supposedly rough neighbor- hoods in New York or Chicago, my parents always taught me that the West Side was different. Teenagers mill about in front of the site of the former Jewish Theological Seminary across the street. *You go there and you get yourself killed.*

Come on, Paula, let's get in the car.

"All right, let's see if any of those places are still standing," Paula says to me, then finally winds up her phone conversation and gets into the driver's seat of her car.

We begin by looking for her father's old apartments. The neigh- borhood still seems bleak. Kids stand on street corners, but none sit on the front stoops of the houses or the apartment buildings. Near the Eisenhower Expressway, we do pass a familiar-looking business.

"Maybe your dad lived in that Starbucks over there," Paula says.

The night is hot. Kids on bikes wheel around an abandoned Amoco station. Streets curve into cul-de-sacs or they just dead-end. The Starbucks is empty, too. A sign in the window says it's going out of business.

Paula drives slowly toward Homan Avenue. "Left or right?" she asks.

"Left," I say. But when we get there, her grandparents' home at 704 Homan seems to be either a new low-income condo building or a housing project.

"Strike one," I say.

"Should I go back the other way on Homan?"

"Try the next street."

We pass the Faith Community Baptist Church—more kids hanging out, brownstones in states of disrepair. Cars parked on the street have been reconstituted from junk parts—a black door on a white car.

"Now I understand why my parents don't like my charming vintage apartment in Chicago," Paula says. "It's because of what it reminds them of. It reminds them of when they were poor."

"Apartments with plastic on the furniture," I say, remembering. "I grew up with lots of plastic on the furniture."

"We didn't have it in our house, but all our grandparents had the plastic," says Paula. "That's one of my earliest memories, sitting on my grandmother's couch in the summer with no air conditioning, sitting on the plastic."

"Sometimes the plastic would rip and I'd get scrapes on my legs," I say. "Then we got rid of the plastic, but we couldn't just sit directly on the couch, because it would get dirty, so my mother put tablecloths on the couches, and my father put plastic Con-Tact paper on the kitchen table."

"It's poignant when you think about it," says Paula. "They worked so hard to have nice things; it's not taken lightly to have a nice couch, a nice table."

"What are we looking for, 604?" I ask.

No 604, either, only a fast-food restaurant where it once stood: Wings 'n' Things.

"Strike two," Paula says.

Paula and I tick sites off our list so quickly that I call my mom just to see if any of the places where she lived are still around. My mom and I haven't been discussing the Bonus March much lately; ever since my father got sick, she hasn't liked talking about the past—it's all *nuchum*, she usually says, something that's gone, and futile and depressing to try to recapture it. Still, she gives me an address on Jackson Boulevard, not far from Garfield Park, where she and her sisters used to sleep on some hot summer nights. Nothing there, either, just an empty lot. Paula turns the car around, heads back south.

"What are we looking for now?"

"3801 Harrison."

Harrison, where Paula's grandfather's old butcher shop once stood, runs parallel to the Douglas elevated train line and alongside the Eisenhower. We see a cracked, potholed street, empty factories with glass-brick windows, and gates pulled across doorways before we start looking for another one of Paula's dad's apartments.

"I wish we could see just one of the actual places," I say.

"But at least this gives a physical reality to stuff that's been ethereal," says Paula.

"Did you ever ask your father to take you around?" I ask.

"I might have, but he would say, 'Ahh, there's nothin' there.' "

"Sounds like my dad. Where did your mom grow up?"

"In the equivalent area of Milwaukee, where everything from her life is torn down."

"Have you gone back there?"

"No, it's just the same thing; everything's torn down."

"Is this Independence Boulevard again?" I ask. "Does this go two ways? Oh, there it is. Your dad's place is now Maxwell Street Polish Hot Dogs."

The sun is beginning to set, and it seems as if just about all signs of our parents' early youth are gone. If there really is a key to opening up any secret about my father's past, I don't think I'll find it in the neighborhood where he grew up.

"Wow," Paula says. "Out of five, we found zero."

"Let's get back on the expressway," I say.

IV

A cool rain falls as I walk through what remains of my father's professional world. I cross South Wood Street, where my my mom used to work at the Illinois Neuropsychiatric Institute, past the old University of Illinois radiology department, its hallways and stairwells still the same battleship gray I remember from the few times I accompanied my dad there. I walk around the block, then onto Paulina Street. I walk through the administrators' parking lot, past the good space that was reserved for my dad, then through long, fluorescent-lighted hallways and on into dark rooms, where radiologists' faces are dimly illuminated by the light that passes through the X-rays they read. It's a surprisingly long walk from my father's old parking space to the radiology department, but my father did it every weekday until he was in his late seventies. Sometimes he had trouble walking from the living room to the kitchen in our house, but he could always tap some inner reserve of energy to make it to work.

Here in the radiology department, the atmosphere is quiet and studious, more redolent of the world of letters than that of medicine. The hallways outside are filled with the rumble of gurneys, the beeping of medical equipment, the quick, purposeful footsteps of doctors and nurses, the moans of patients, a cacophony of conversations. But here, where the radiologists read their X-rays, all is comparatively calm; talk between doctors is hushed, as if by mutual agreement. Patients are out of sight—they are in the other rooms, down the hallways, up the stairs, their life stories conveyed here through images, not words.

Other than the house on Mozart Street, this was probably the most important place in my father's life when I knew him. But less than a decade after he retired, there's little sign he was ever here. Pictures and plaques on walls are reserved for former department heads. Few people are left here who worked with my dad. One radiologist, the silver-haired Ray DesRosiers, saw him only in his last years and remembers mostly the difficulties my dad had walking the hallways. "I never did see him slow up, though," DesRosiers says.

Teresa Zamarron, a health center administrator, worked with my father for twenty years and remembers his drive and his dedication.

"Oh, would he push me," she says with a laugh. "If I didn't have films ready for him, he would call me and say, 'I have nothing to do.' That was the worst thing for him—to have nothing to do."

"One of the advantages your father may have seen in being a radiologist is that you're never someone's primary doctor," says my dad's former resident and colleague Dr. Andy Wilbur, who still works here. "You don't have that responsibility."

Since my father retired, some of the equipment at the U of I has been updated—the contents of the file room are being digitized; no one gets to work quite as early as my dad used to and no one leaves as early as he did, either. The requirements of the job have changed somewhat, too—there's more emphasis on collegiality, the ability to work together to divvy up the load. Reading CT scans and MRIs, a skill my father chose not to learn, is now required, and usually calls for more interface with patients. In this era, it's harder to keep your distance.

My father's tiny, windowless office, which he shared with Andy Wilbur, is still here, though. My dad used to sit in it when he needed to give his eyes a rest. The best thing you could do for him when he sat in that office, says Wilbur, was to bring him a Coke, then give him his time by himself.

I thought my father might have been a different man at his office, but no, his colleagues all describe the man I knew—fast, driven, focused, no chitchat, as distanced from his colleagues as he usually was from me. I remember that when I was in kindergarten and I didn't care for some of my classmates sitting at my table, my father advised me to behave like Greta Garbo: *I vant to be alone.*

"He never really wanted a lot of discussion," Dr. Wilbur says. "Sometimes you'd be talking to him and he'd start saying, 'Well . . . all right . . . ' and you'd sense he was really saying, 'All right, move it along.' That's how he was with everybody."

"But your father was lucky in a way," says Wilbur. "He got to do what he was good at."

1976

For my father, the story of the Bonus March may have been one of futility, and that's a reasonable way of looking at it if you stop with the first march in 1932 and don't keep going until 1936, when the bonus bill passed. But for me, it is one of admirable perseverance—of destitute, malnourished men continuing to march around the Capitol even after the Senate defeated their bill, of veterans returning to Washington year after year to demand the money and respect they felt the government owed them. And if I could isolate one thing I learned from my father, it is that intense drive, that strong will to always move forward, whether or not anybody else was following.

I'm in fourth grade now, and I'm still a fairly sheltered kid. One of my favorite toys is a manual Royal typewriter, on which I write mysteries or plagiarize biographies of NFL running backs. My brother and sister are the only baby-sitters I've ever had. I get rides to and from the private school in Evanston where I've transferred from the Chicago public schools—Mrs. Kraft's de facto independent-study math class at Boone Elementary, in which second graders had to line up in order to receive any instruction at all, put my mother over the edge.

I have a yellow Schwinn that came with a removable crossbar so that it can serve as either a girl's or boy's bike. I ride the bike a lot, but only on the sidewalks and rarely anywhere except around and around my block. Whenever I stray too far from Mozart Street, some big kid invariably yells, "Girl's bike! Girl's bike!" because my dad never bothered to put on the crossbar, and then I speed home as fast as I can.

Tonight, it's raining—hard. We're over at my aunt Faye's house for dinner. Faye is my mom's older sister, and her late husband, Harry, used to run a store on Western Avenue near this South Side neighborhood of Mt. Greenwood. We come here for dinner a lot.

Over the course of the evening, the rain gets even harder—a real downpour. Tornadoes have touched down on the South Side of Chicago and the civil defense alarms have been blaring. Then the power goes out. On 114th Street, where my aunt lives, there are no curbs, and the streets and sidewalks are filling with water. I go outside, my pants rolled up, and, like every other kid playing in the street, I walk barefoot and splash through the downpour. My cousins are going down to their basement to get army cots so that everybody can sleep here, because it's far too dangerous to drive.

As a family, we have never slept over at any friend's or relative's house, and to me, the prospect of doing so sounds like incredible fun; I might even get to miss part of school tomorrow. But past midnight, the moment the rain begins to let up ever so slightly, my father is already heading out to the car, and soon we get in with him. We drive through the flooded streets, my father's car kicking up water as we head slowly but purposefully to the highway. One way or another, my dad's moving on, getting home; he won't sleep anywhere except in his own bed, and nothing is going to stop him.

JEROME

I'm now in Skokie, Illinois, visiting the man who knew my dad longer than any other living person. My uncle Jerome Langer was my dad's only sibling, and I'm sitting in his backyard, talking to him and his wife, Donna, a retired schoolteacher, about the Bonus March book my dad wanted to write and what it might have meant to him. But Jerome says, "We don't know about that. He never talked about it to us." Donna adds, "Your dad wasn't a talker," and Jerome says, "No, he wasn't. No no no."

My dad and his younger brother were born a year and a half apart, both were bar mitzvahed at B'nai Reuben Synagogue, and used the same teffilin I would use forty years later at my own Bar Mitzvah; they went to the same grammar and high schools, lived together in the New Lawrence Hotel when my dad was in med school and my uncle was in law school, before Jerome got into the steel business. My uncle gave my dad his first car, a 1950 Pontiac; my uncle now drives my dad's last car, a 2001 Crown Vic. The two brothers married Jewish gals and had three kids apiece, Jerome's oldest one year younger than my brother, Jerome's youngest a couple of years older than I. Except for the time when my father was in college or when my uncle was in the military, Jerome and my dad never really lived more than four miles from each other.

But I'm not surprised that my dad never discussed his book with my uncle. It would be hard for me to imagine brothers so close in age and geography yet so far apart in personality—my father, the clean-shaven, quick-witted, acerbic intellectual physician with the house in Chicago; my uncle, the gregarious, fast-talking, goateed Atlas Steel salesman with the house in the Chicago suburbs and the condo in Florida. My dad's humor could be nasty and dark—once when we were sitting shiva here at Jerome's house for a relative, my dad struck up a conversation with a car salesman whom he considered a shyster, trying to see if he could get the guy to talk business even at this solemn event. That was my dad's kind of humor, a private joke at someone else's expense, and I don't think he minded when people around him were staring—the shame of it, trying to cut a deal on a Honda during shiva. My uncle's patter, on the other hand, often sounds like that of a Borscht Belt comic.

"Your uncle is a sharp businessman," Sheldon Schoneberg, a Marshall High classmate of my dad and uncle, has told me. "He'd sell you the oil company. Your father and his compatriots were not businesspeople at all; we were schleppers."

Now retired, Jerome goes to men's club meetings at the Northbrook Court shopping mall and raves about the quality of the lox at their bagel brunches; my dad never joined any men's club, or any other club for that matter. Jerome is the pack rat, and his wife keeps telling him he needs to get rid of more stuff; my father kept little from his past: a photograph, the stamp album he gave me, his rain-damaged high school annual, which he kept in one of his old barium barrels—that was about it.

My father stayed in school during World War II; after graduating from Marshall, Jerome enlisted in the U.S. Army Air Force. When my dad was in college at the U of I, Jerome was stationed downstate at the Chanute Air Force Base, in Rantoul, Illinois, after which he served in Japan. Even Jerome's and my father's vocabulary and manner of speaking were different. When he is having trouble remembering something, Jerome's speech is equal parts Kojak and Martin Scorsese: "I'm eighty now, baby," he says. "It's hard to remember so many things."

I ask if Jerome thinks he and his brother had much in common; Jerome says no. But Jerome has little problem with saying that my dad was the smarter of the two, the artistic one, too, the one Jerome would call upon to help with homework, to draw sketches for class-room assignments.

"I wasn't a real good student. I was medium," he says, recalling a teacher named Mrs. Lee, who taught both of them at Marshall High. " 'You're not as good as your brother,' Mrs. Lee said. So help me God, she said that, and it still sticks in my mind," says Jerome.

What the two brothers did have in common was that ability to persevere. Jerome suffers from diabetes, has hearing aids in both ears, he's now older than my dad was when he died, and yet here he is, still pushing forward, gardening, driving to medical appointments, to concerts to see his grandson Andrew perform with his band the Sleeptalkers. Jerome and my dad also shared an exceedingly sharp memory and a Chicagoan's distinctive penchant for remembering places not in terms of street corners or neighborhoods, but specific addresses: "We lived on 1626 S. Springfield and then we moved to 1815 S. Avers. Then we went to 4161 Fifth Avenue."

The family moved to Fifth Avenue, Jerome says, because their apartment on Avers was on the third floor and my dad had trouble walking the stairs. "In those days, your father was very severely handicapped," Jerome says. "For a time, he walked with crutches and it was hard for him to navigate, and my folks took him to different hospitals. They took him to Illinois Research Hospital. There was a Dr. Thomas who wanted to operate on Seymour, but the way I heard it was that if they operated on him, he might not have been able to walk at all. So it was a decision for my folks to make—operate or not. They decided not to."

Jerome pauses. "He probably never told you that," he says.

Nope. That's one of the stories my dad left out.

The image of my father as a child in and out of hospitals, walking on crutches, does not match any of the colorful West Side childhood stories my father ever told me, or the only picture I have seen from my dad's early years—a framed black-and-white eight-by-ten shot of a placid five-year-old sitting astride a tricycle. The photograph is still mounted on a wall in the Mozart Street basement. Were it not for the boy's black lace-up shoes and the style of the tricycle—front wheel twice as large as the rear pair—I could be easily convinced it is a photo of me.

Jerome's earliest memories of growing up in Chicago coincide with the time of the Bonus March, but he recalls only the basic facts of that episode. He doesn't remember his father marching to Washington, or considering marching to Washington, or even discussing the incident with him or my dad. Instead, he recounts a lively childhood during the Depression, which didn't affect their family as much as it affected others—say those who were living in tents on the Anacostia Flats, awaiting more food donations whenever supplies ran out, contracting diphtheria and tetanus from the tainted water there.

"We always had plenty of food, always had a car," Jerome says.

"One car we had was a used Packard that had been used as a limousine. I liked that car, because when we had to deliver an order on the way home, we could put six to eight cases of pop in it."

Jerome remembers Sam Langer attending the Galicianer Synagogue, but he says that the family wasn't particularly religious—they couldn't afford to be; their biggest pop delivery day was Saturday. On Fridays, my grandmother Becky Langer would wash the floors and afterward put down newspaper. Later, when my dad was in med school, my uncle would take her to the hospital, where she was being treated for breast cancer, from which she would pass away at the age of fifty. "She made challahs, she made a coffee cake, and we had chicken; I can't remember anything else."

"Did you ever know my dad to be interested in writing?"

"No, never said one word about it."

"Was he a big reader?"

"When we were growing up, he was always studying. But I don't know what he was reading."

"Did the studying rub off on you at all?"

"No, no, no."

"Did it ever seem to you that he was studying too much?"

"I don't know. It could be. Who knows? Certain things I don't remember at all."

"Was the way he walked something other kids accepted?"

"Not too much. They accepted Seymour because Seymour was Seymour—a nice guy, smart, industrious. But I can't say it wasn't a hindrance."

"Did you have to be protective of him?"

"I don't remember."

As I sit with Jerome and Donna in their backyard, our conversation punctuated by the sounds of lawn mowers and locusts, my uncle and aunt engage in the well-practiced repartee that comes with more than fifty years of marriage: Jerome talks; Donna adds information; Jerome agrees or needles her with a smart remark.

"Your grandfather's family was very family-orientated," Donna says. "They didn't go out to restaurants. They went to each other's homes and that's how they spent the weekend."

"We used to go, the whole family," says Jerome. "We'd go straight out west, uncles, aunts, cousins, straight out west there on Roosevelt Road, and there was a grove where we had picnics."

"They had family outings," says Donna. "They were always at somebody's house. Did they play cards?"

"No," Jerome says, "but we're trying to talk about Seymour now."

"Yeah, but I heard you talking," says Donna, "and that's what the family used to do. They weren't like people now. They didn't run to movies or restaurants. They loaded up the truck and went out to the country."

Still, if Jerome has any further insights into my dad's past or his family or why he might have been interested in an obscure incident in American history, he doesn't let on. Jerome rarely denies a story, but he doesn't confirm many, either. When I recount a story that doesn't jibe with his own memories, he rarely says "No," just "Could be." Jerome remembers that my father was born Sidney Langer and the name was changed to Seymour, but says he doesn't remember why. He remembers my grandfather said he had worked as a bartender, but my uncle never heard about the speakeasy in Al Capone's Levee District. And if Sam Langer ever mentioned he fought in World War I or served as a mule skinner then, Jerome doesn't remember that, either.

"Could be, yeah," he says.

"Was there a General Langer who fought the Russians for the Polish army?"

"Could be, sure."

I ask if Izzy Tuchman (no relation to Barbara, by the way), the baker from Leonard's Bakery, really delivered speeches at Bughouse Square.

"Could be. Izzy was that way."

Jerome remembers working jobs in high school—for Henrici's restaurant, for the post office as a special-delivery boy, and at Lytton's men's store, but he doesn't remember my father working for the *Chicago American* or anyplace else in high school, save for the pop factory. Jerome remembers the holdup that took place there. "Your father was there and they made him lie on the ground. He was mad because he had white pants on." But he doesn't recall the dog named Troubles that got shot in the robbery.

Jerome can't confirm where his parents came from, either. Though he says he has a copy of my grandfather's immigration papers, indicating when Sam Langer came over from Langerdorf, Austria, after we go into his house and start looking through his boxes, we can't find it. What we do find are photos from Jerome's service years in Japan and afterward; he has very few of my dad or their parents. "Who had cameras back then?" He tells me he'll look harder for the immigration papers; if he finds them, he'll call me.

"I wish I could tell you more, but I just can't," Jerome says. "Tell you the truth, I just don't remember all that much and I don't know how much I ever knew. In those days, you didn't ask. Your dad and I came from an era when parents didn't talk too much to their kids about personal things."

1977–78

I'm ten years old and I'm a third-year gimel student in Mr. Nathan's class at K.I.N.S. Hebrew School in West Rogers Park, and I'm one of the only Jewish students in Ms. Mandell's sixth-grade class at

Baker Demonstration School in Evanston. Ms. Mandell is a hip young teacher who sometimes talks to us about her dates. She consults us about whether she should go out with "Dan the detective" or a man named Chet. Our class has voted for Chet because he has the same name as White Sox outfielder Chet Lemon.

Ms. Mandell has taught us the bus stop, the tango hustle, the Chicago walk, and the other disco dances she's learned at a singles club called Faces. She has lectured us about women's lib, refers to our principal as a "male chauvinist pig," and insists we call her female student teachers Ms., not Miss or Mrs. She is also the first Jewish grade-school teacher I've had at this private school.

Ms. Mandell has just recently begun talking to our class about the Holocaust, something I haven't heard about before. For a while, I have known that there must be some reason why my family doesn't buy German products and why I could have Legos and Erector sets but nothing made by fischertechnik. My parents have never told me the reason, and I've never asked.

In Ms. Mandell's class, we've been instructed to write reports on TV shows, and I've written an extensive critique of a new family comedy called *Eight Is Enough*. In the spring of 1978, Ms. Mandell tells us about a television miniseries called *Holocaust* that is going to be broadcast. She wants the whole class to watch it and write reports. She has asked us to pay special attention to an actor named Michael Moriarty, who plays a Nazi and is, she says, the best actor in America.

In my Hebrew school class, we've been discussing the miniseries, too. Mr. Nathan has told us that every Jew has a relative who died in the Holocaust; every American Jew has a relative who didn't make it out.

That night, at the dinner table, I ask my father if any of our relatives died in the Holocaust. "No," he tells me. I tell him that Mr. Nathan has said that every Jew has a relative who didn't make it out. "No," my father says, "every one of your relatives made it out."

PEPI

Born in 1922, my father's first cousin Pepi Bernstein tells me that my grandfather might well have served in World War I, but she saw a lot of my father's family during the 1930s, and if there were any extended pilgrimages to Washington, D.C., for the Bonus March or any other reason, she probably would have known about them. Whenever I talk to my relatives such as Pepi, and I mention my grandfather, they say nothing about the military; they talk only about how hard he worked, how busy he was, how many cases of soda pop and seltzer water he could carry when he was on a delivery run.

In 1932, veterans may have been selling apples in the Chicago Loop at a stand on the corner of Jackson and LaSalle streets, for instance, but Sam wasn't one of them. Elsewhere, unemployed army veterans were piling into trucks bound for Washington, D.C., but no one remembers Sam Langer ever being out of a job, and the farthest away that anyone remembers him traveling was to South Haven or Union Pier, Michigan, for weekend family getaways.

"I'm the oldest living relative now," Pepi tells me, but she still has a sharp memory—one way you can tell is by how much she claims to have forgotten. The people I've met whose memories are failing don't seem to know how much they're supposed to remember.

"My memory of those years is fading," Pepi says. "It's not that I'm bad. For my age, I'm very good, but I have forgotten a lot of things, and it aggravates me. That's how it is, though. You get older and you can't remember."

We're sitting with Pepi's boxes of photos, news clippings, and memorabilia—that is, limited-edition gold-rimmed plates with Lionel Barrymore's etchings on them. We're on the couch in the living room of Pepi's apartment in the condominium complex Winston

Towers. I once nicknamed the complex "Cabrini-Greenberg" because it resembles Chicago's once-infamous Cabrini-Green housing project, save for the fact that it is populated mostly by elderly Jews. Winston Towers is located on the northwest side of Chicago, and Pepi has lived here by herself ever since her husband, George, passed away about fifteen years ago from an infection that Pepi believes may have been the result of the shrapnel wound he got when he was with the marines during the Battle of Okinawa in World War II. Pepi's mother, Bessie Cohen, was my grandmother's sister, and my dad always said Pepi was one of his favorite relatives; Pepi speaks with a similar fondness for him and for my grandfather, who, she says, was her "favorite uncle." A "precious man," she tells me.

"I got pictures plenty," Pepi tells me as she hauls out a photo album.

Indeed. There's dapper and mustachioed Dr. Lou Bulmash, Pepi's late brother-in-law and also my childhood dentist, who used to try to take my mind off extractions by turning the station of his black-and-white TV in his California Avenue office to the show *Shazam!* There's my grandfather's brother Alec Langer, who worked for the Goldblatt's Department Stores chain. He is pictured with his second wife, Sophie, who was, Pepi says, a "very showy woman." Both—an anomaly for Jews and Chicagoans—were active in the Republican party in the 1940s and 1950s. "I'm a very devout Democrat," Pepi confides. "I'm a Democrat and I want what's good for people. I'm not a Republican. I never have been, I never will be, and neither are my children."

Here at a table at an anniversary party is Sol Langer, another of my grandfather's brothers, who worked as a fruit peddler on Chicago's South Side. "Sol sold fruits and vegetables and then he also worked for Goldblatt's. What can I tell you about Sol? Bessie, his wife, who was also my father's sister, was supposed to get married to this guy and he jilted her and so she latched onto Sol, so Sol's wife was my father's sister and Sol Langer was my mother's brother and Uncle Sam's brother. You got that?"

Some of the best pictures in Pepi's collection are those of Pepi herself as a teenager, dressed for work as a waitress at her mom's diner; she looks like a smart, sassy, gum-cracking lass out of an early Hollywood talkie like *The Petrified Forest*. "All I did was pose," she says, and quickly rummages past those photos, looking for others. "If I see one more of these pictures, I'm gonna kill myself. You can have it; I've only got a dozen of 'em. I'm just sick. I'm absolutely sick. The pictures that I want to find, I'm not finding."

Finally, she says, "Look, here's Dad," and hands me a photo. It's my father on the tricycle again, the same photo that's in my parents' basement, still the only childhood photo of my dad I have ever seen. A normal kid, a normal childhood, no crutches. The photo he clearly wanted me to see, the story he wanted to tell, with the unpleasant parts left out. Just a normal kid, the way he most probably wanted me to think of myself, too, and the way I nearly always did.

"I remember something about your dad," Pepi tells me. "When things weren't goin' his way, he used to lay down on the floor and kick with his feet. Oh, was he hot when he was a baby, but he turned out to be a terrific guy."

Pepi spent her earliest years on the West Side, where she lived with her parents and her sister and brother, Bee and Harold. They moved all the way north to the somewhat more affluent Jewish enclave of Albany Park, but when she was nine, her father, who worked in the produce business, died after he was struck by a train, and she and her family moved back to the West Side.

"She had to make a living," Pepi says of her mother, who, following her husband's death, operated Bessie's Diner in a produce-auction area at Fourteenth Street and Western Avenue. The diner was in a retired Illinois Central railcar on the watermelon track, then later on the potato and onion track. It had a copper floor and about two dozen stools. The rail company gave the train car to Pepi's mother as part of a settlement following the death of Pepi's dad.

Because Pepi's mother was a widow, she and Pepi spent a lot of time with my father's family. My uncle Jerome taught Pepi how to ride a bike; Pepi helped my grandmother make butter cookies. "A great gal," Pepi says of Becky Langer. And as for Sam Langer, whenever there was a family outing in the park or the forest preserves, he made sure that Pepi and her mom came along.

Pepi began working in the diner when she was eleven. "We had a very popular place," she says. "A lot of sophisticated men who worked on the train and brokers would all come into our restaurant. We washed plenty of dishes, and our place was as clean as can be." During the summers, Pepi would get up at 3:30 A.M. and leave the diner at about 3:00 P.M.; her mom would close up afterward. "It was no bed of roses, believe me," she says. "We didn't have a car; we used to get on the streetcar to go to work. Oh boy, that was somethin'. My mother had a guy who used to bring meat to the house, and we would carry the meat down to the diner on the streetcar. And then we would have to carry it under a viaduct, and it was plenty scary carrying the stuff at five o'clock in the morning. Thank God we never had any trouble. Sometimes if my mother would go on a vacation, I would have to go by myself in the dark, and that wasn't so great."

Pepi remembers having only two outfits back in those days— a cotton dress with wide pleats, which she wore during warm weather, and a green-and-gold blouse and a green skirt, which she wore in the winter and would wash and press every day after she got home.

"I'm sure that other people had more, but I didn't have a father, so we did what we could," she says.

Pepi worked for the diner until she turned twenty-five and her husband, George, returned from the marines to work for his family business, Ogden Oil. From there, the story becomes more familiar to me—suburbs, children, a granddaughter. The only times I really ever saw Pepi were at weddings, Bar Mitzvahs, and funerals, and when she would come over to our table at Myron & Phil's steak house. The last time I saw her was at Shalom Memorial Park for my dad's funeral.

"I remember telling you how sorry I was that I hadn't seen him more," Pepi says. "It wasn't his choice any more than it was mine—we just didn't do it, that's all."

As I speak with Pepi, I see that, in a way, nearly the entire history of my father's generation and the twentieth-century Jewish American experience is contained within the stories and keepsakes of this eighty-some-year-old woman on the northwest side of Chicago. Here in the old-country photos of Fanny Tarshis, née Cohen, and my grandmother Rebecca is the story of immigrants journeying from Eastern Europe to Ellis Island to pursue the American Dream; here in the pictures of Bessie's Diner is the story of Jewish life during the Depression; here in George Bernstein's letters, and the letters that her brother-in-law sent to her when George was in the hospital, are the World War II stories: "Pearl, I am glad that George's wound has fully recovered. They can't keep us Bernsteins down, can they? George is a tech sergeant and that is pretty good money, but there is not enough money made to pay the boys for what they go through."

"Would you look at this," Pepi says as she scans the letter. "It's like history."

All that's missing really is the Holocaust, which somehow my father's ancestors managed to survive.

At the bottom of Pepi's picture box are photos of relatives from Eastern Europe—a portrait of my grandmother as a young woman, a photo of Pepi's aunt Fanny Cohen, and of two other siblings, a brother named Moises and a sister whose name was Pepi, too.

"But they perished during the war," says Pepi Bernstein.

"What?" I ask.

"They never made it over."

But my father told me that all of our relatives made it out, I say.

"No," Pepi says. "One of your grandfather's brothers and one of his sisters, they didn't make it out."

"My dad never mentioned them," I say. "He left that part out."

"He probably didn't want you to know," says Pepi. "It's not a good story."

No, my parents didn't want me to hear those sorts of stories. I didn't hear about my father on crutches, didn't hear about a Moises or a Pepi who didn't make it over. I heard inspiring rags-to-riches tales of Sammy Berkman inventing Kayo and Harry Bell owning hotels, heroic stories of a General Langer fighting the Russians for the Polish army.

"Well, I'm sorry I haven't been more helpful," Pepi says as she and I begin to put back her pictures. "I'm here in this apartment thirty-nine years. Where have the years gone? My husband has been gone fifteen years. I cannot believe it. I should believe it. I do believe it. But you blink your eyes and I can't believe I'm eighty-five years old. When you're eighty-five, you'll remember your cousin Pepi Bernstein said, 'Where did the years go?' and she was right."

1978

I'm still in sixth grade, on spring vacation. Before our class left for two weeks, one of our student teachers gave us a take-home questionnaire about how we want to lead our lives when we grow up. One of the questions is about friendship. Would we like to have one best friend? Two or three good friends? Or just many friends? This is the question I am still pondering, because I find myself unable to choose; I want all of the above. I like talking to friends on the phone for hours, like talking to my brother about the Chicago White Sox, to my sister about college, to my mother about books she's reading or stories I'm writing. I don't talk to my father all that much, though.

Sometimes, when the weather is warm enough, we sit together on the front porch. My dad with his military histories; I read my Madeleine L'Engle books, but I don't ask him many questions. I somehow feel that I'm not supposed to. It's hard for me to keep up with him. For a while, he was trying to teach me how to sketch, but drawing is one of my worst subjects, and I could sense his impatience.

One Saturday afternoon, my friend Phil comes over to my house. When we hang out, we play Wiffle ball, listen to Groucho Marx and Stan Freberg records, build models, make crank telephone calls, and devise ideas for original games that we've been submitting to companies such as Parker Brothers and Cadaco. This day, we take a walk around my neighborhood, and as we do, Phil seems subdued. I don't ask what's wrong, but he tells me anyway—his dad has been working on his taxes and he'll have to pay another eight hundred dollars to the government.

I have little concept of money. I don't have an allowance, but I do understand that my father can be a generous man. Once, when we had an extra ticket to an Arthur Rubinstein piano recital, my father gave away the ticket, even after someone offered to give us one hundred dollars for it. He gives to the Jewish United Fund, and when I ask, he donates to my charities of choice—the Jacques Cousteau Society and the National Wildlife Federation. "It's only money," he likes to say. And if I do ask my father for a few bucks to spend on baseball cards or records, he gives it to me. But pretty much the greatest expenditure I've asked to make is $8.49 for the Rolling Stones' *Hot Rocks* double album at Record City, so eight hundred dollars sounds like a lot to me.

That night at dinner, after Phil goes home, I tell my dad about Phil's father's predicament and ask if eight hundred dollars is a lot to pay in taxes. My father says it is. Then I ask my dad how much he pays in taxes.

"That's not your business," he says. And I am beginning to understand that there are topics that I can discuss with other people but that I cannot discuss with my dad, details that he will not disclose, information he will leave out of his stories. I resolve not to ask him about money again. Still, I feel glad that I have best friends, good friends, and many friends to talk to, and that I don't have to choose only one of the above.

IRA

My father's first cousin Ira Bell lives with his second wife, Claire Pensyl, in their Wilmette house, where the two of them also run their law practice. Ira grew up in Uptown on the North Side of Chicago, not far from Uncle Harry Bell's New Lawrence Hotel. A gray-bearded man with a sharp, self-deprecating wit and an easy guffaw, Ira is the son of a furrier named Benny and a seamstress named Ida, whom I remember from my childhood, when she was already a widow, living alone in Winston Towers. Even now, I can still hear her Yiddish accent, a link to the old country and my history that had nearly disappeared by the time I became conscious of it. Ida offered a hint of what my grandparents' voices might have sounded like.

Ira was born more than ten years after my dad, and three years after the Bonus March, and he's too young to remember seeing the pop factory, though he says he does remember hearing stories of fights that broke out there between my grandfather and my father's uncle Phil Bell, a tremendously skilled but uneducated cabinetmaker. The story Ira heard ended with one of the men whipping a bottle at the other.

As the University of Chicago–educated lawyer who handled much of the family business and was the go-to guy when my dad's health began to fail and he started to consider making a will, Ira knows a lot of family stories. When I mention to him that my dad had talked about wanting to write a book, Ira says, "Oh sure, I remember him talking about it."

"You remember him talking about wanting to write it?" I ask.

"Yeah, I remember him mentioning it."

"That's great," I say. "Did he ever tell you why he was interested in the Bonus March? Do you remember what he said about it?"

"The what?"

"The Bonus March."

"What was the Bonus March?"

I explain. But Ira says my dad never discussed writing the Bonus March book with him.

"What book did he tell you he wanted to write?"

"He said he wanted to write a book about the Haymarket Riot."

"What did he say about that book?"

"He said he was working on it and he had already done some research."

"Did he talk about it any more than that?"

"No."

Sure, I've heard about the 1866 Haymarket Riot in Chicago, when a bomb was thrown at police during a labor rally and eight anarchists were arrested. They were tried for the crime, and four were later executed. It's another one of those overlooked, marginal stories about underdogs that my father enjoyed telling, and its futile ending is similar to that of the Bonus March story my father told me. Unlike the Bonus March, the Haymarket Riot is commemorated by a plaque, which is located on Randolph and Des Plaines streets in Chicago. But my father never told me about the incident, and he certainly never mentioned writing a book about it to me. It must have been one of those stories he told once or twice, then forgot shortly after proposing it. According to Ira, though, many of my dad's stories were not completely true.

No, Uncle Harry Bell was not quite the *macher* my father claimed, Ira says, not the real money behind my cousin Sammy Berkman's Bio-Science Laboratories. "Everybody always believed that," Ira says, "but when I handled Uncle Harry's estate, I discovered that what we had been told about him was so far from the truth. He did well, but the impression that he was a kingmaker was grossly exaggerated."

My father said that Uncle Harry Bell owned the New Lawrence and the Edgewater hotels. Not true, either, says Ira.

"I represented the family when they sold the hotel," says Ira. "Uncle Harry promoted the deal, but he was not the big money behind it."

"Was Sam Berkman chairman of the board at Dow Chemical?"

"Not that I know of. Think about it. A Jew being chairman of the board of Dow Chemical? That would be like having a Jewish Pope. It's possible, but I don't think it's gonna happen."

"Did he invent Kayo?"

"Not that I know of. Are you putting me on now? Maybe the rumors are better than the real stories."

1978

I'm almost eleven, and lately I've been assuming that my father's profession will become my own. At school, when one of our teachers asked us to come up with topics for oral reports, my suggestion was "Diseases of the Chest." My father has been recommending books that he hopes will continue to inspire me to become a physician— *Microbe Hunters,* by Paul de Kruif; *Arrowsmith,* by Sinclair Lewis; *A Surgeon's World,* by Max Thorek; *The Citadel,* by A. J. Cronin.

I've even started to read military history and have been writing espionage-themed short stories inspired by William Stevenson's *A Man Called Intrepid.*

Other members of my family are less impressed with my reading list. My brother, who's in medical school at the University of Illinois and studying to become a radiologist, like our father, rolls his eyes when I boast that I've just finished the William Stevenson book. "Great, so you're Einstein," he says. My mother smiles with pride and regret when I tell her what I've been reading. "So you're not going to read any more kids' books?" she asks. "You'll miss out on an awful lot." Nevertheless, I can see my future fairly clearly: I'm going to read X-rays and books about war and spies.

Today, I've been shopping with my mom at Armanetti's Liquors on Western Avenue. To my mind, this must be the most boring store in the history of the human race. I sometimes come here with my brother and gaze blankly at containers of cheese dip and bottles of Canfield's soda pop while he contemplates which wine to choose for Sunday family dinner. This afternoon, I'm accompanying my mom while she looks for a white wine to go with the coquilles St. Jacques she'll be cooking.

Outside in the parking lot, a man has collapsed and can't get up. He's probably in his sixties, and he says that he lives at the nursing home nearby. My mother tries to help him, but he is big and it takes just about all her strength to get him off the asphalt and onto an embankment. My mother spends about a half hour waiting with the man for the paramedics to arrive. My dad is parked on Western, and though he gets out briefly to check on the man, he soon gets back in his car and stays there. I go to the car and ask if he's going to offer further medical assistance, but my father says no. I ask why not—doesn't he feel sorry for the man?

"I feel bad for him, sure," he tells me. "But, look, he smells of booze and he was on his way to the liquor store."

I get in the car and sit with my father, and we watch my mother sitting beside the man. It feels strange sitting and watching from the car when my mother is out there, but I don't say anything. I just sit with my dad. We wait for the doctor and the paramedics to arrive.

For Memorial Day weekend of the same year, I fly with my parents from Chicago to San Francisco. This is the only occasion, in my recollection, when I ever traveled with just my mother and father, and the last trip I would ever take with my dad. I'm sitting between my mom and dad when a flight attendant makes an announcement over the intercom: "We have a problem in first class. If there is a doctor on board, could he please come to the first-class cabin?"

A tall man with glasses and wavy dark brown hair gets up and starts moving quickly from the main cabin to first class. I expect that my dad will follow suit—there's an emergency and someone needs medical aid. But my dad stays put.

I ask why he's not getting up, and when he doesn't say anything, I try to make sense of why he isn't moving. I ask him if he thinks doing so would be pretentious.

"Yeah," he says; he wouldn't want to call that much attention to himself.

I don't say anything more, but my father's answer sticks with me all through the trip and afterward. By now, I'm beginning to question whether I do really want to be a radiologist. I'm squeamish about blood, though, and am not sure what other kind of medicine I could practice. And I wonder whether I might not become a doctor after all.

SAMMY

The more I've been learning about the stories my father told, the more I've been questioning even the ones I haven't heard debunked—though my father's birth certificate confirms that his name was changed from Sidney to Seymour, I wonder if fooling the dybbuk had anything to do with it. I wonder, too, if there really was a relative in the Polish army who fended off the Russians during World War One. That story in particular always sounded bogus. Uncle Harry Bell didn't own the New Lawrence Hotel; the Bonus March story didn't end in 1932. The stories are always more complicated, the endings less clear-cut. Still, the story of my cousin Sam Berkman was one of my favorites, and I have trouble letting go of it. The way I understood it, his was a true American Dream tale of a kid growing up poor to immigrant parents, then making good.

"I don't know what 'made good' means," Sam Berkman tells me. Born in 1916 and now retired in Beverly Hills, he seems to have little patience for my chitchat. "I assume by 'made good,' you're talking financially."

Well, yes, of course the money was part of the story, I say, but it was about more than that, more than the fact that Sammy wrote a big check for my Bar Mitzvah gift in 1980, more than the fact that Sammy became a major donor to the University of Chicago and gave one of their libraries his first-edition art books. Sammy seemed to typify the tales I enjoyed of struggle, striving, and ultimate triumph. He made his way from the Old West Side, where he lived with his brother Irv and sister Lily across the street from their family delicatessen on Trumbull Avenue, while his parents lived behind a partition in back of the store. He worked for my grandfather at S & L Beverages and ultimately moved to California: "I walked into the jungle . . . And by God I was rich."

But Sam, a laconic speaker, says he has no great nostalgia for the Chicago of his past. His West Side in the 1930s was not the rich, colorful Jewish neighborhood that my father's stories conjured up for me, but one he was more than ready to leave.

"I'm a little surprised to hear you have the impression that the West Side was idyllic," he says. "That's not my recollection of the West Side and not my recollection of your father's reaction to the West Side."

S & L Beverages, where Sammy worked in the office, barely deserved to be called a factory, he says. S & L operated out of a building that my grandfather, along with Phil Bell and the man named Segal, got cheap from a company that had gone broke, and it was probably too big for the soda-pop operation, whose products, according to Sam, were hardly remarkable. The one memorable detail about the pop business, says Sammy, is the fact that its red delivery truck had solid rubber wheels.

"But that place was a mess, believe me," he says. "It wasn't managed well at all. Everybody went his own way. There were nothing but arguments. The three of them did not get along at all. It was not a good operation. I didn't have to be older or wiser to know that. You'd have to see that place to believe it existed. It was a small outfit run in the old-fashioned way, which means there was no system of any kind."

Sammy remembers nothing of my grandfather Sam Langer's war service, nothing of the Bonus March, but he recalls Sam Langer as a hardworking but somewhat "eccentric" man, meaning that even when Sammy Berkman was a teenager, he noted that my grandfather would "do things in a way that I wouldn't do them."

Although Sam talked to my father many times throughout his life, what he remembers most about my dad was his ability to cope with his difficulty in walking. "Your father had great courage," he says. "He was severely physically handicapped and he never let that bother him. He was in and out of the hospital, but he seemed to keep his composure. He was never bitter, as far as I can remember. I didn't see how he could be as nice as he was being as physically handicapped as he was. I had a lot of respect for him because I don't believe I could have done what he did with the problems he had."

My father's story that Sam Berkman invented the Kayo chocolate drink is sadly false, though. While he was a graduate student at the University of Chicago, Sam worked as a consultant for Aaron Pashkow, who ran the Chocolate Products Company and invented Kayo. But Pashkow invented Kayo in 1929, long before Sam worked for the company. Sam's work for Chocolate Products involved trying to develop ways to use sweeteners such as beet sugar to make soft drinks during sugar rationing. "We made a lot of progress, but we didn't get any patents out of it," Sam says.

As for the story about Sam's being chairman of the board of Dow, it really goes like this: During World War II, Sam Berkman worked in the Sanitary Corps with the 227th Station Hospital in the Pacific theater, and became a major, spending time in the Philippines, New Guinea, and South Korea. After his discharge, he worked in the chemical-warfare division of the U.S. Army at Camp Detrick, Maryland, remaining there for almost two years before deciding with some buddies to open a laboratory. The business was named Bio-Science Laboratories, and it became a phenomenal success story. According to Sam, it was the largest lab in the world and had branches in Germany, Canada, Brazil, and Japan, before ultimately being sold to Dow Chemical in 1973. But as for Sam Berkman serving as chairman of the board or even on the board of Dow, Sammy says, "Not likely, no."

"I'm surprised that the stories were exaggerated by people other than myself," Sam says now. "I can understand if I were the one to exaggerate. I'm not prone to exaggerate, but usually the person being talked about is the one who exaggerates."

But how did the myths develop? I ask. And what did it say about my father that he created this image of Sammy's success? Was it a desire to invent a larger-than-life story, some inspirational family myth? And might not that also have something to do with my father's focus on the Bonus March, a need to equate his own family story with something larger and more universal?

"Let me ask you something," says Sammy. "Is it in your nature to talk this fast?"

"I guess so," I say.

"Let me give you a piece of advice," he says. "You talk too fast."

1980

My Bar Mitzvah reception is being held in a ballroom on the second floor of the Drake Hotel, and it's far too opulent for my tastes—an open bar, a band, filet mignon for dinner, coffee ice cream rolled in chocolate chips and plopped in Kahlúa for dessert. My father has told me and my mother that the medical outfit for which he has been reading X-rays might be going out of business soon, which makes me feel even less comfortable with the money my folks are shelling out. My parents have given me a camera as a Bar Mitzvah present, which makes me feel guilty, too; I wonder if I should return the gift in case my father will soon be out of a job.

For the reception, my parents have vetoed my idea of renting a 16-mm projector and screening my favorite movie, *Casablanca*—just about all of my favorite movies were made during my parents' youths. I have vetoed their (well, my mother's) idea of having me play a Mozart sonata on the piano for what I imagined would be the collective horror and boredom of my relatives and friends, most of whom are away at summer camp anyway. Sure, Ellen Rich is here, but what difference does that make? She already has a boyfriend; I saw them kiss during the snowball dance at her Bat Mitzvah at the Sovereign Hotel. My favorite drama teacher, Lali Morris, is here, too, but what difference does that make? She's ten years older than I am and she has a boyfriend with a thick black beard.

At the reception, I spend much time sitting in red-cushioned window seats, sneaking whiskey sours, and telling dirty jokes with the few friends of mine who are here. Before dinner, my father gets up to give a speech. He speaks of how quickly time passes—just the other day was his Bar Mitzvah, and soon I will be up here speaking for my son's Bar Mitzvah, and he wants to invite everyone here to my son's Bar Mitzvah. Everybody applauds; I applaud, too. But something strikes me as slightly wrong about the speech. In our conversations, my father has never spoken in this eloquent and sentimental manner, and he has never discussed his Bar Mitzvah with me. And since I've yet to have a girlfriend, I'm not particularly convinced I'll ever have a son, and if I do, whether he'll even have a Bar Mitzvah, and if he does, how many of these people will still be around.

My cousin Irv Berkman, the steel salesman, is here; so is my cousin Marvin Reiner, a car salesman; also in attendance is Sabine Bell, widow of the legendary Harry Bell. As it will turn out, none will be alive to attend my hypothetical son's Bar Mitzvah, even though they were there when my father stood up to offer his invitation. At least, I'm pretty sure they were there, although I can't be absolutely certain, for these memories exist solely in my mind and in a handful of photographs; only about a dozen pictures were taken at the Bar Mitzvah, because my father said he didn't want to hire a photographer. I sensed that he really didn't think the event was worth recording. The only pictures are the ones I took with my new Canon camera, most of them blurry and dim because I was working without a flash; the pictures of me are taken in a mirror. Even now at my Bar Mitzvah, I have already learned that if anyone tells the story of me and my family, it will probably be me.

THE SINGERS

By now, I've heard enough stories that I'm not surprised when I learn that my father's cousin Izzy Tuchman probably never spoke out about communism at Bughouse Square.

"I don't think my father ever did that," says Izzy's daughter Pepi.

"He was with the union a little bit," says Pepi's husband, Jerry, "but he wasn't very vocal."

"Nothing to do with politics really," says Pepi.

As it turns out, there were four Pepis on my father's side of the family—Pepi Bernstein; Pepi Singer; Pepi Reiner, who supposedly used to have the best memory of anyone in the family but is now suffering from memory loss; and the Pepi who didn't make it over from the old country. The history and state of my father's generation can be told in the life stories of women named Pepi.

Pepi and Jerry Singer live in Skokie, down the street from my uncle Jerome. Pepi was born in 1929, and she and Jerry have lived here for nearly fifty years, far longer than they lived on the old West Side. And yet their street—quiet, safe, suburban—doesn't feel much like part of a neighborhood to me. Jerry agrees and says he blames the ubiquity of the automobile.

"You know what was unique about the old West Side?" he asks as I sit at the little kitchen table across from him and his wife. "Ninety percent of the people who lived there did not have cars. As kids, we had to walk. I lived on Sixteenth Street, but I used to walk to Twelfth Street so I could hang out at Nadler's Poolroom. We knew so many people, and there was a closeness that I don't think you kids were ever exposed to. When we leave the house here, we get into our car, and we're gone. With our kids, we had to send them to camps in order for them to have friends to play with. The unavailability of the car made the West Side what it was."

Jerry Singer should know. After he got out of the military service in the 1940s, he spent his professional life in the car business. He and my father's cousin Jack Tarshis owned the Highland Park dealership where my father bought every one of his black Fords. "He always got a new car, and it was always black," says Jerry. For his part, my father was available for medical advice whenever Jerry and Pepi needed it.

"Your dad was Johnny-on-the-spot," Jerry says.

When she was growing up on the West Side, Pepi lived with her parents, but since her father left the house before dawn to get to the bakery, when her mother was giving birth or her brother was ill with spinal meningitis, she stayed with my dad and his family.

"Aunt Becky and Uncle Sam were very good to me. Especially with making cookies," Pepi recalls. "Your grandmother was just a nice Jewish woman—loving, sweet, that's what you remember."

"Pepi was thrown around a little bit as a youngster, pushed from place to place," says Jerry. "She always talked about how well your grandmother treated her."

"What do you remember about my grandfather?" I ask. "My father said he was a mule skinner in World War One."

"I don't remember that. I don't think so," says Pepi.

"I don't recall him ever saying he was in the service, honestly," says Jerry. "That story may be fiction."

Fiction. Yes, I think so, too. I wonder how much more of what little my father told me will turn out to be fiction.

What Pepi and Jerry do remember are the family picnics, the Yiddish conversations about the old country, the gatherings they'd have with my parents in their East Rogers Park apartment shortly after my folks were married, the *simchas* and the funerals where they would see my mom and dad, the times they would meet my folks at Myron & Phil's. Pepi remembers my father on crutches as a kid, but mostly she and Jerry remember my dad's generosity with medical advice and his intelligence.

"If I recall, your dad was the valedictorian of his class in high school," says Jerry Singer. "To be the valedictorian of your class, you really had to be something special."

Actually, the valedictorian of my father's graduating class at Marshall was a kid named Marvin Lehtman. But I don't contradict Jerry; even though it's fiction, it's a nice story. The myth is inspirational and comforting. My father exaggerated stories about his relatives and friends, and apparently they embellish the stories they tell about him, too.

JOHNSTOWN, PENNSYLVANIA

Road-tripping from Indiana to New York with my dog, I check into a motel outside Johnstown. In that town, many members of the Bonus Army who had been kicked out of Washington camped at an amusement park, before their onetime ally, Mayor Eddie Mc-Closkey, a hotheaded former prizefighter, told them they were no longer welcome: "For God's sake, take this gasoline and the dollar bill and be on your way!" For the better part of a week, several thousand veterans and their families slept near the merry-go-round and lighted swimming pool of Ideal Park. They pitched makeshift tents near the tires of their roadsters.

Finding evidence of their brief stay here is tough. The town is now most notable for the movies that were shot here in the 1970s and 1980s—*Slap Shot*, filmed partly at the Cambria County War Memorial Arena, where Republican vice presidential candidate Sarah Palin held a 2008 rally, and 1983's *All the Right Moves*, in which high school footballer Tom Cruise griped, "Now, you can't even get a job in that damn mill."

Ideal Park is now an outdoor soccer field. The Cambria County Public Library has only a half dozen or so articles in its archives about the marchers, most from the Johnstown *Tribune-Democrat*. Still, the headlines of these stories do a fairly good job of summarizing the story of the Bonus vets here: BONUS ARMY DESCENDING ON JOHNSTOWN; FIELD HEADQUARTERS OF KHAKI SHIRTS TO BE ESTABLISHED HERE; SEMI-CHAOTIC CONDITIONS AT IDEAL PARK CAMP; BONUS ARMY WORE OUT JOHNSTOWN'S WELCOME. Even less is available at the Johnstown Area Heritage Association.

In the morning while I'm checking out of my motel, I ask the woman working at the front desk if she knows anything about the marchers' stay at Ideal Park, which in 1932 was nicknamed "Camp McCloskey."

"I sure don't," she says.

Then I ask her if the town might have at least some kind of memorial or other commemoration. She now smiles with recognition.

"Oh sure," she tells me, "but actually, the site isn't in Johnstown; it's about ten miles away, in South Fork."

"Really?" I say. "This is the first I've ever heard of a memorial."

"Well, a lot of people come through town to see it," she says. When she was a girl, she went with a school class.

"So people around here know the history?" I ask. "They learn about the Bonus Army in schools?"

"*The what?*"

"The Bonus Army."

Oh, no, she doesn't know anything about that, she says; she was talking about the 1899 Johnstown Flood.

1981

I'm a freshman at Evanston Township High School and I'm over at the house of my friend Andy, whose dad, Seymour Levine, attended high school with my father. Although I've been writing a lot—derivative, melodramatic plays based on shows I saw with my mom and brother on a trip to London, and semiautobiographical, probably libelous fiction based on my experiences at Hebrew school—I've been continuing to consider a career in medicine. I'm on the "Accelerated Science" track at ETHS, and whenever anyone asks me what I will be when I'm an adult, I'm still saying, "A radiologist."

We're in the living room before dinner and one of Sy Levine's relatives tells me she knows my father. "Oh," she says, "you must be Seymour's son." It's a perfectly banal and accurate remark, but at that moment, I realize that, no, I really will not be a radiologist or any other sort of doctor; I know that I won't be as good as my father, and I think now, for the first time, I really don't want to be known as "Seymour's son."

II

Stories We Create

To this day, no one has ever heard him admit that he could not walk. Never have his crippled legs deterred him from going where he would.

TIME magazine on the subject of
Franklin Delano Roosevelt, 1933

1982

Now a junior in high school, I feel as though I have little in common with my father. We barely ever spend time with just each other. This year, when my brother and my mom were out of town, my dad and I saw a movie together at the Will Rogers Theatre, but I felt distracted the whole time. For some reason, I kept having a premonition that my brother and mother would perish in a plane crash, and, since I'm the only kid still living at home, I wondered how I would cope living with just my dad.

I've given up my plans for a medical career and have become a lousy science student. Unlike in English and history classes, in which I do just fine, my writing ability has little value here; I cannot BS my way through a chemical equation. Completely unprepared for a test in Dr. Taylor's class, I blow it off but later am shocked to learn that Taylor, despite the fact that he seemed to be a laid-back wisenheimer, will not let me retake it and will instead give me a zero, something that has never happened to me before.

In a panic, I ask my father if he'll write a letter on my behalf, protesting Dr. Taylor's decision. My dad tells me to write the letter myself on his stationery and he'll sign it. So, channeling what I feel to be my father's voice, I write a terse, angry letter, reminding Dr. Taylor of his responsibilities as a high school teacher. My father briefly reads it, signs it, and I hand it to Dr. Taylor at the beginning of the next class. While I'm working with my lab partners on an experiment, I see Dr. Taylor mutter to himself as he reads my letter. Then he comes over to me and asks if I've read the letter. I shrug, then lie. No, I tell him, my dad just put it in an envelope and told me to give it to my teacher. How dare my father lecture him about his responsibilities? Dr. Taylor asks, and storms away to his office. I hear him dial a phone, then leave a message for my dad. During the next few classes, Dr. Taylor makes wisecracks about my father. "Maybe we need the opinion of a real doctor on this one; let's call Adam's dad."

But at the end of the week, without having gotten in touch with my father, Dr. Taylor begins to relent and tells me I can retake the exam. And over the course of the rest of the year, Dr. Taylor adopts a kinder tone with me, sensing, I presume, that it must be rough to grow up with the pompous, demanding author of the letter he received. I want to tell him that my father's not really all that much like the man I've portrayed on paper. But I don't say anything to Dr. Taylor; I just listen to him mock the pretentious, curmudgeonly dad I have invented.

NEW YORK

I

After they were forced out of Washington, D.C., then Johnstown, Pennsylvania, the veterans of the Bonus Army began to drift and spread out. Plans were made to establish colonies for the veterans in such locations as Waterbury, Maryland, and Mexico, but those plans were scuttled by the governor of Maryland and the president of Mexico, both of whom had more than enough to contend with, given their own homeless and jobless populations. In Chicago, about seven hundred veterans found temporary shelter in a brick house on West Pearson Street, where they lived on bread and beans before the fire department declared the building dangerous and forced them to leave.

In New York, veterans tried to sleep in City Hall Park, found emergency shelter on Greene Street, and attempted to camp in the Lower Reservoir in Central Park, which had been drained previously. Makeshift villages and tent cities emerged near factories. In Riverside Park, some former members of the Bonus Army, tired of spending nights in missions and relatives' houses, pitched tents between the railroad tracks and the Hudson River opposite Seventy-fourth and Seventy-fifth streets. The marchers christened their homes with ironic or comical names—"Grand Hotel," "Rain Inn," "The House That Jack Built." In *To Have and Have Not*, Ernest Hemingway wrote of old veterans in Riverside Park offering to let passersby urinate in their beards for a dollar. In 1933, at the Heckscher Foundation's auditorium on Fifth Avenue at 104th Street, the Jewish Workers' Theatre performed a Yiddish translation of Charles Walker and Paul Peter's play *The Third Parade*, which was about the Bonus Army.

But today, no plaques are here to mark the New York parks, lots, and rail yards where the veterans slept. There is no Glassford Avenue in Riverside Park anymore to honor the D.C. police chief, nor is there any street in the city named after a Bonus Army marcher. The sites of the veterans' Riverside Park dwellings are near where I take my dog for walks or my daughter to the swings and slides in the playgrounds. No shantytowns along the East River, no "Packing Box City" on Houston Street, no "Hard Luckville" on East Tenth Street, no tin city in Central Park across from the nursery school where my wife and I walk with our daughter every weekday morning. Nannies push strollers along park paths where a little more than seventy-five years ago, veterans used wood fires to cook whatever donations they'd scrounged up—leftover pies, rations of meat and potatoes. Today, Whole Foods stands at Columbus Circle, where in 1932 eight hundred veterans began marching down to the West Twenty-third Street ferry, bound for Jersey City, where they would try to hop a train to D.C.

II

The actor Reathel Bean has appeared on soap operas and in TV dramas; he has played small roles in such feature films as *Cocktail* and *The Nanny Diaries.* On Broadway, he was news anchorman Roland Headley in *Doonesbury.* But back in the heyday of the Off-Off-Broadway theater scene, Bean frequently performed in shows at the Judson Memorial Church, led by writer-composer Al Carmines, who was an assistant minister at the church. In 1976, Carmines wrote the music and lyrics for a musical entitled *The Bonus Army,* helmed by Jacques Levy, with a book by David Epstein.

The musical, a lively piece of agitprop reminiscent in its best moments of Marc Blitzstein's *The Cradle Will Rock,* seems as if it was intended as a corrective to Bicentennial patriotism. It sympathized with the marchers, while presenting the members of the Hoover administration and the American military as buffoons. "I'm just a poor boy who did it all himself / And like every member of the G.O.P. / I ask myself through many a sleepless night / Why can't everybody be like me," Hoover sang in the song "An American Success Story."

Critical response was tepid. In the *Soho Weekly,* Gerald Rabkin remarked, "The piece covers predictable ground which unfortunately trivializes the plight of the marchers." And in *The Villager,* Cynthia Lee Jenner complained that "there's never any doubt who the good guys and the bad guys are; it's as clear as in a Hopalong Cassidy western."

Today, the musical exists only in a few script copies and in tinny cassette recordings. The script I found was in the Judson Memorial Church Archive in the Bobst Library of New York University. "It probably wasn't as good as we thought," says Bean, who played one of the marchers. Though there were hopes the show would transfer from the Judson Memorial Church to a more professional Off-Broadway venue, Bean says the musical didn't extend beyond its planned three-week run.

At the end of the show, the Bonus Army sang "One More Day" ("Keep our hopes alive / Work and pray / When our dreams all come true / Just the way we want them to. / We'll be glad that we waited / One more day"), and for Reathel Bean, the dim hopes and the persistence of those Bonus Army marchers mirrored the lives of actors in a show that would never make it to Broadway—working, striving to be heard, hoping their struggles would pay dividends, yet all too aware their efforts would probably be in vain.

"Yes," says Bean now, "all of us were destined for oblivion."

III

On the day I walk from my Upper West Side apartment to the East Side digs of Norman Podhoretz, former editor in chief of *Commentary* magazine, I've been considering which particular political aspect of the Bonus March might have made my dad want to write about it. My father did like military biographies, but when he described the Bonus March to me, Douglas MacArthur always seemed like the villain. My dad couldn't have been on Herbert Hoover's side; like most Jews, he seemed to be a Roosevelt man. Still, other than make some clever PR moves (such as having Eleanor meet the Bonus Army marchers and sing "There's a Long, Long Trail" with them when they returned to Washington in 1933), FDR didn't do much more for the marchers than Hoover had. And when the bonus bill finally passed in 1936, it did so over Roosevelt's veto.

The march became a cause célèbre for the so-called radicals who tried to infiltrate the movement, but my dad was hardly the protesting type; I never heard him take sides on any contentious issues in or just before my time—Vietnam, nuclear proliferation, apartheid. He distrusted ideologues and politicians; most were "schmucks" in his book.

Like many Jewish men of his generation, my father started out on the Left. But also like many Jewish men of his generation, he didn't stay there. He claimed that in 1948, in the first presidential election in which he was eligible to vote, he pulled the lever for neither Thomas Dewey nor Harry S. Truman, but for Socialist candidate Norman Thomas, who ran in every presidential election from 1928 to 1948 and who, in his 1932 campaign, supported the Bonus Army, speaking in Brooklyn's Ulmer Park to denounce Hoover shortly after the marchers had fled D.C.

But when I knew my dad, the only times he got involved in political discussions were when he delivered quips—of a wealthy fellow Marshall student with revolutionary leanings, he once remarked, "The schmuck was the only one who could afford a revolution." He would opine about the desirability of a benevolent despotism, or he would quote Winston Churchill on the subject of democracy ("the worst form of Government except for all those other forms that have been tried from time to time"). At one family gathering, my father informed my aunt Roz Herstein that normally he would take into serious consideration her insistence that we boycott Dow Chemical for its involvement in manufacturing Agent Orange but for the fact that he owned stock in the company (he didn't). My dad worked for the city's Municipal Tuberculosis Sanitarium during the first Mayor Richard Daley's administration and, following the death of Mayor Harold Washington, said he was being courted as a possible commissioner of health by one of his former students, who was married to a mayoral candidate. But my dad told me he wasn't interested in the gig—political jobs didn't pay enough and there was little job security after Richard J. Daley died.

My dad seemed to like Adlai Stevenson and John F. Kennedy, but later he spoke highly of Barry Goldwater, mostly because of his Jewish roots. In the 1970s, he became an avid reader of *Commentary*, frequently recommending Norman Podhoretz articles to me. And in 1980, my dad voted for Ronald Reagan. Or at least that's what he told me.

When I meet Norman Podhoretz and his wife, Midge Decter, author of *Rumsfeld: A Personal Portrait*, among other books, parallels with my dad are obvious. Born in 1930 to a working-class Jewish immigrant family, Podhoretz began as an ardent leftist. In the 1948 election, he was too young to vote, but he supported Communist candidate Henry Wallace. *Commentary* began on the Left but moved toward the Right in the late 1960s. And in 1980, though he says he usually tried to stay above partisan politics, Podhoretz did, for the first time, cast a vote for the Republican candidate, Ronald Reagan. Podhoretz even resembles my father in that he's a smallish, sharp-witted Jewish man who begins some of his sentences with "In any event." If I can't interview my father anymore, at least I can get some insight by talking to someone who reminds me of him.

"Your father's story is very much like mine," Podhoretz says.

In Podhoretz's apartment, I avoid discussion of two issues. The first is that this is not the only time I've encountered his wife, who is wearing a *Saturday Night Live* sweatshirt (her daughter-in-law's a producer of the show) when she greets me. When I was a senior in college and I'd long since concluded my brief flirtation with conservatism, which largely consisted of contributing a restaurant review to the campus's fledgling right-wing newspaper, I stood up at a Decter speech to challenge her. "You're contradicting yourself," I bellowed, after which some campus radicals pumped their fists and shouted "Yeah!" But whatever I was trying to say was convoluted, and the campus radicals began muttering loudly before I was through. Decter said something sharp and nasty and shut me up.

The other point I avoid mentioning to Podhoretz is that my dad cast his last vote in 2004 by absentee ballot for John Kerry.

"It was a gradual process. It was not a *Road to Damascus* bolt of lightning," Podhoretz says of his own conversion to conservatism, which he uses to attempt an explanation of my father's political development. "A lot of thought went into it, a process of rethinking a lot of old ideas and conceptions."

Podhoretz says his rightward shift began following the Six-Day War of 1967, when he started to see a growing anti-Americanism and anti-Semitism on the Left, often disguised, Podhoretz says, as anti-Zionism. "You began to hear really vile things about Israel connected with what Jews were doing to people of color," he explains.

"I would guess your father must have been affected by these same forces and influenced by some of the arguments we were making, because we were very effective critics of the Left—we knew the Left, we had been there, we knew their vulnerabilities, and we knew what people said during unguarded moments. We knew how to hurt," Podhoretz says. "I imagine that for somebody like your father, especially of his generation, our arguments would have been very persuasive."

As for the Bonus March, Podhoretz theorizes that my dad might have been intrigued by the fact that the incident "showed Roosevelt in a different light." People on the Left always regarded MacArthur and his ilk as fascists, Podhoretz maintains, but Roosevelt was, and still is, greatly admired by Jews, who, he says, often overlook the fact that FDR passed up the opportunity to bomb the train tracks leading to Auschwitz.

"The Jewish worship of Roosevelt was based on an illusion," Podhoretz says. "But these myths persist, and I don't know whether they will ever be overcome."

In the time I spend with Podhoretz in his apartment, I keep listening for my father's voice, trying to find more resonances or contradictions, wondering whether my father's interest in the Bonus March really did have anything to do with FDR, particularly since the story he told ended in futility before Roosevelt became president. And as Podhoretz and I talk, I do feel as though I'm doing something my father would approve of, something he would have boasted about and probably exaggerated to his liberal friends: *Did I tell you Podhoretz had Adam over for dinner? Did I tell you Adam's gonna be writin' for Podhoretz?* My dad was the one, after all, who tried, albeit unsuccessfully, to talk me into applying for an internship at William F. Buckley's *National Review*. "Just send them your résumé; you can always say no," he told me.

But then I try to imagine my dad in this room. What would he say to Norman Podhoretz? I wonder. What would the two men discuss? Not until I'm almost done chatting with Podhoretz and I ask if he thinks my father's biography mirrors that of a typical *Commentary* subscriber do I finally hear my father's voice. But when I do, it's not saying what I expected it to.

"Well," Podhoretz says by way of a response, "among most American Jews, many regard me as a villain. But there is a group which has startled me. Lately, everywhere I've gone, after I've finished talking and I'm signing books, people will come up to me and say, 'You changed my life,' and it's very gratifying. So, if your father was one of those, I seem to have met at least a hundred of them in the past few weeks."

At first, I don't make much of this remark, so I don't say anything. But the more I turn Podhoretz's statement over in my brain, the more I begin to think, No, actually I can't imagine my father as "one of those." He never asked anyone to sign his books, rarely attended speeches or author readings; Isaac Bashevis Singer's and George Steiner's were the only ones I can recall. And I'm certain he would have resented being called an acolyte by anyone, even Podhoretz. My father always relished having contrary opinions, which was probably a big reason why he read Podhoretz's magazine in the first place. The moment Norman Podhoretz declared him to be "one of those," I could imagine my dad canceling his subscription to *Commentary* and signing up for *The Nation* or telling Podhoretz he had voted for John Kerry.

If your father was one of those . . .

What would my father do or say at this point? I wonder. Would he stay to argue the point? Would he keep silent and stew? Would he make some cutting remark? I stay on the couch and keep talking with Podhoretz, but as I do, I can imagine my father getting up, then walking fast to the door. *I'm gonna go get the car,* I can hear him saying.

SENATOR JOHN KERRY

"Well, your dad didn't come full circle, but he came half circle," says Senator John F. Kerry with a wry smile when I tell him my father cast his last vote for him in 2004. "He didn't make it all the way back to Norman Thomas. But, wow, I'm really touched."

My father distrusted politicians, and his 2004 vote was mostly a vote against George Bush, but Kerry was the sort of man my father would seem to have liked well enough—intelligent, erudite, serious. Of all contemporary politicians, with the possible exception of Pennsylvania senator Arlen Specter, who wrote that his decision to go into politics was influenced by the Bonus March and the experiences of his father, a Great War vet ("In a figurative sense, I have been on my way to Washington ever since to collect my father's bonus," Specter has written), Kerry is the one whose life story draws a direct line from the struggles of veterans seventy-five years ago to those of today. Plus, as I'm sure my father knew when he was putting an *X* by John Kerry's name on his ballot, Kerry's grandfather was born Jewish; just about anyone with Jewish ancestors was okay in my dad's book.

Outside, in the waiting room in Senator Kerry's office in the Russell Senate Office Building, one staffer has been taking a meeting with lobbyists for Merck & Co., while another is strutting into the room to ask for a signature on a letter she wants to send out. On the walls are photos of Kerry as a Swift boat captain, in a hockey uniform, shaking hands with dignitaries, speaking before the Senate Foreign Relations Committee, in perhaps his most memorable political appearance in 1971, when he uttered the quote that became an anthem for the disenfranchised soldier: "How can you ask a man to be the last man to die for a mistake?"

Kerry, silver-haired, regal, with his familiarly equine features and a disarming penchant for greeting visitors with a handshake, a backslap, and a clubby and stentorian "Hey, man," is sitting at his desk, while I sit across from him in a leather armchair. I'm wearing a light blue shirt that was my father's and a red tie with gray clouds on it that also belonged to my dad. Kerry's chief of staff takes notes as the senator tells me the Bonus March had long been a part of his consciousness, even before he returned from Vietnam.

"I had the historical memory of veterans coming to Washington to voice their grievances and camping out," he says. "The idea of camping came directly from the Bonus March. I'd read about it for history classes and I was struck by the impact it had at the time; I was also struck by the fact that veterans had to march simply to get what they thought was coming to them."

I direct the senator's attention to a July 16, 1932, edition of the *B.E.F. News,* the official newspaper of the Bonus Army, featuring an article written by H. L. Mencken, a writer my father admired, who was then editor of the *American Mercury* and whose writings often mirrored my father's fairly cynical worldview: "In the sad aftermath that always follows a great war there is nothing sadder than the surprise of the returned soldiers when they discover that they are regarded generally as public nuisances, and not too honest."

Kerry says he doesn't care for the cynicism of the Mencken quote; still, he agrees that veterans "tend to be forgotten when they come back. We are still having to fight for things that ought to be automatic."

I ask Kerry how much has really changed since 1932, and if sometimes it seems as if he is still fighting the same battles for veterans' rights—doesn't it get discouraging? Kerry says he's "beyond being discouraged," and he points out that the lesson of the Bonus Army is not the one of futility that my father seemed to perceive, but one of perseverance, a quality that my father exemplified throughout his life; after years of struggle, those veterans who survived finally did get what they had been seeking.

"I'm an eternal optimist; otherwise, I wouldn't be keeping at it," he says. "Being discouraged is a self-indulgence. It's annoying. It's frustrating. But when we come back, we can get it done, so in the end, maybe that's our job—to be vigilant, to stay on top of it. That's what they were doing seventy-five years ago and what we have to keep doing."

Toward the end of our conversation, Kerry asks why I think my father was so interested in the Bonus March. I tell him about my grandfather Sam Langer and the story that he was a mule skinner in World War I.

"Well, there you go," Kerry says, as if the mystery has been solved. "It's the service connection."

Afterward, I follow the senator out of his office, and along the way, I ask him to sign a book for a friend of mine back in New York. As I reach for a pen, I feel a small booklet in the inner pocket of my suit jacket. I haven't worn this suit in more than two years and, apparently, I forgot to have it laundered. I pull out the booklet, which comes from Shalom Memorial Park. I received the booklet on the day of my father's funeral, the last time I wore the suit. In the booklet are memorial prayers and one particular prayer to be recited at a father's resting place: "It was my father's desire to raise me a useful person amongst Thy children on earth. Help me to carry out his desire."

I shake Senator Kerry's hand before he walks fast down the hallway, heading toward the Senate floor for a vote.

When I'm back at home in New York, I open my mailbox and find a letter from the Military Personnel Records department of the National Personnel Records Center in St. Louis. The center cannot verify my grandfather's wartime service record, most probably because in July 1973, a fire destroyed thousands of military personnel records. I write a letter to ask if they can use any other method to find out more about my grandfather's service as a mule skinner and my family's connection to World War One. I am still convinced that there must be one.

My Father's Generation: Scene from a Documentary

PART II: THE BULL SESSION

In the 1930s and 1940s, the men and women of my father's generation began to work their way out of the Depression. In Chicago, many such people became the friends who would remain close with my dad throughout much of his life. Some of them left to fight in World War II, while my father stayed behind in school. They lived through the days of the New Deal, began to forge their own careers, started along the road to becoming doctors, lawyers, professors, engineers. Their parents, the contemporaries of the men who had fought in the last war and marched for their bonuses, belonged to a previous generation; their stories were already in the process of being forgotten. Still, I've been asking these people who knew my father about him and about the Bonus March. I am still listening to their voices, still trying to find the connection: What about Rosebud? Don't you think that explains anything? What about the Bonus March? What do you think it might mean?

VOICES: Irv Warso, Sheldon Schoneberg, Mitchell Schorow, Seymour Levine, Bella Stein, Millicent Marks, Lenny Primer, Howard Watt, Norm Budow (Marshall High School, class of 1943); **Jerome Langer** (Marshall High School, class of 1945).

Irv Warso

I really didn't know that much about your dad personally. I don't know what he read or what he wanted to write. I knew him because we had a group. We went to high school together, and we stuck together. What kept us together? Comradeship or something, I don't know.

Sheldon Schoneberg

We had the most interesting relationship, and it still exists today. We don't have to see each other, and as soon as we pick up the phone, it's just like we were with the same person the day before and all the years disappear. I guess we're all in love with each other. We weren't men in love with each other. But we just loved each other. I was closer with those guys than I was with my brothers.

Mitchell Schorow

We were the outcasts. We always considered ourselves outcasts. We took pride in the fact that we were the intelligentsia of Marshall High School.

Seymour Levine

We had a social club back then. We called it the Bull Session. And we used to meet at the Jewish People's Institute.

BELLA STEIN

There were about fifteen or twenty fellows, and they were all good friends. They were nice fellows and they were all pretty square.

MILLICENT MARKS

We had our nucleus of friends that we stayed with all of our high school years. There wasn't a Saturday night that we didn't have a party and it was at each other's homes and it was always the same boys and the same girls and we were just like a pack together.

SHELDON SCHONEBERG

We didn't really do anything. We were typical West Side guys. We were just a little nutty; we weren't hoodlums; we didn't even smoke or drink. We'd joke around, go to an occasional movie, have a weekly meeting at the Jewish People's Institute. They'd have a dance upstairs and we'd go up and stand around and say, "Should we ask a girl to dance?" But we never did; that was too brave for us.

SEYMOUR LEVINE

Mainly, we ran around and fooled around and talked about girls. We never really had a formal agenda. The big thing was trying to figure out where we were gonna eat—"Where do you wanna eat?" A lot of times we wound up at Benny Kane's Barbecue on Fifth Avenue near Harrison Street.

LENNY PRIMER

I don't even know what the hell we talked about. It was just an excuse to get together. We had meetings at the Jewish People's Institute on Wednesday nights. They had a big night there at the JPI, and we once put on a production of *Ferdinand the Bull*. When we would leave, we would all walk out the front door and we would walk down Douglas Boulevard to Central Park Avenue, and your father would get on the bus to go home. When he'd get on, all twelve or fifteen of us would yell,

"Hello! Goodbye!" as if he were going on a trip. He'd be so embarrassed, but we'd do it all the time. That was really cute.

SHELDON SCHONEBERG

We were constantly insulting each other in a nice way. It's like the comedians that you see from the Borscht Belt and from Chicago, like Shecky Greene, who was also a West Side boy. Everybody gives everybody a little dirty dig. In fact, one of ours, Larry Gelbart, became a great comedian. We used to put on shows. We both dressed up as Mandarin Chinese and we had to stage an act for the high school. I thought I was funnier than Larry Gelbart back then.

LENNY PRIMER

We did crazy things. There was a program on the radio called "Lights Out," with Arch Oboler. We'd turn out all the lights, and the voice-over would go, "Ghost stories! Weird stories! And murders, too! Heh heh heh!" And they'd tell an Arch Oboler story, and it was supposed to be scary, and you know what we'd do? We'd jump on each other and wrestle in the dark. Isn't that crazy?

IRV WARSO

We had a friend of ours, Alvin Michel. His father was a cabdriver. He lived on Grenshaw Street and he had an old Pontiac, and one night we got in it, and we picked up fourteen guys and put them in the Pontiac, drove downtown to the Chicago Theatre, and in front of the theater, all fourteen guys got out. Your father came along.

LENNY PRIMER

We stacked I don't know how many people, drove to the Chicago Theatre, and everybody started coming out like clowns at a circus.

IRV WARSO

Then the war came.

HOWARD WATT

I was down at the U of I with your father when the war got going. It was a big university and just about everybody down there was in ROTC, including me, and they drafted people. I was rejected, but within a couple weeks, they had practically emptied out the place. They sent a lot of them out to the Pacific, where they were slaughtered.

JEROME LANGER

I didn't want to go to the infantry, so when I was in high school, I took an exam and passed. I could have gone to the Navy V-12 program or the air corps. I couldn't swim, so I enlisted in the air corps. When Seymour was going to school downstate, I was stationed at Chanute Air Force Base. And I used to come in quite often to get meals. And when I'd come back to Chicago, I'd always bring cigarettes for our uncle Sol. During World War Two, you couldn't get good cigarettes. You couldn't get a brand name; you got shit—Raneses or something. Sol couldn't wait till I got home—not for me, for the cigarettes.

NORM BUDOW

I was in the signal unit, climbing up telephone poles and working on telephone lines. The poles were kind of chewed up, and I was climbing one and I fell down about twenty-five feet and broke my leg, so I was in an army hospital when my unit was shipped overseas. They threw me in the military police and I was supposed to go overseas with them, but then Germany surrendered, and so I didn't have to go there, either. They were going to ship us to the Pacific theater, and then Japan heard we were coming and they surrendered and I didn't have to go there. You can say I was lucky or unlucky that I didn't have to go.

LENNY PRIMER

When I was in the service, we picked up our plane in Terre Haute, Indiana, and we flew down to West Palm Beach, Florida. We were going overseas and it was winter and we had a two-engine airplane and we flew so slowly, you could have knocked us down with a spitball. There were nineteen airplanes in our group, and they didn't tell us where we were going. An hour and a half after you take off and you lose sight of land, you open up the sealed orders like you do in the movies and they tell you where you're headed. Our plane wound up headed for a bomber base in England. Seventeen planes went to Karachi, India, and out of those that went to Karachi, eighty percent of them were killed. It's a flip of a coin who lives and who dies. All life is like that, I guess. Isn't that something? At the time, I didn't know.

Howard Watt

One of our group, Harold Visotsky, was taken into the army. He was about five foot six, brilliant, became chairman of the department of psychiatry at Northwestern University. But he was a little squirt. Still, he ended up getting a battlefield commission. The army was segregated, and back then, blacks were always used in transportation—backbreaking stuff. Toward the end of the war, they did make some black companies, and the blacks were very anxious to fight. They ended up in the Bulge, and Harold volunteered to lead a patrol—three or four black guys, and Harold as an officer. Harold and his group went out on a reconnaissance mission and they saw a German group coming toward them and Harold saw a German throw a "potato masher" at him—a grenade. Harold got hit. The four black guys turned around, killed every member of the German patrol, picked up Harold, brought him back. He ended up with a terrible head injury and he received everything except the Medal of Honor.

Norm Budow

A kid named Seymour Kaufman was part of our group, and he had terrible vision, wore these pop-bottle glasses. But he was full of the old piss and vinegar, wanted to fight fascism and so forth. Somehow, he got into the infantry, and when they scaled the cliffs of Normandy, he was just cut in half. His mother was devastated. They sent her the life-insurance check and she wouldn't even open it up. "It's blood money," she said.

LENNY PRIMER

Do I think it bothered your father that he didn't serve? Sure, I think it bothered a lot of people who didn't. If you didn't serve, you were considered a draft dodger or a guy who wasn't working. Nowadays, nobody wants to go to Iraq; nobody wanted to go to Vietnam, and justifiably so. But at that time, we knew we were the good guys and that was the difference. Sure, it bothered people.

(*Pause*)

Did he ever tell you it bothered him?

NORM

If my father discussed his Bonus March project with anybody outside my immediate family, it surely would have been Norman Budow. Norm met my dad when both were five years old and lived in the same building on the old West Side. They attended grammar school together, then Marshall High School, where both were members of the social group they called the Bull Session.

Norm was always one of my favorites of my dad's friends—a fiery, effusive, leftist World War II veteran and a professor of U.S. and Latin American history at Truman College, in Chicago. He attended, and still attends, antiwar rallies with his wife, Bess, and was writing letters to the editor of the *Chicago Tribune* back in 1954, protesting the American excursion into Indochina: "Yours is the only daily newspaper in Chicago with courage enough to publicize Dulles' plans to trade our American boys' blood for Indo-Chinese rubber and tin. Keep fighting for America." In early 2007, the Associated Press photographed Norm wearing a NO WAR! button on his hat and applauding a resolution to impeach George W. Bush.

125

When I knew them, most members of my dad's Bull Session posse were already settled like my dad was. Their great American journey seemed to be just about complete. They had houses in safe neighborhoods on the North Side of Chicago or in the suburbs, yards out front, air hockey and foosball tables in the basement, garages with two or three cars in them, rec rooms where kids had more toys than they needed, more records and tapes than they could ever play. Norm was the only one who suggested to me what life on the West Side might have been like. He'd ride his bike with its upright handlebars over to Mozart Street, knock on our door or ring the bell, come inside for dinner or just to chew the fat with my dad, then pedal home to south Evanston.

Many of my father's best old West Side stories involved Norm, who says his French teacher at Marshall High gave him an A for "academics" and an F for "comportment." There were lots of stories: the time Norm was fooling around with nitroglycerin in his family's house and the windows shattered and his aunt admonished him in her heavy Yiddish accent: "Norman, the living room just exploded!"; the time a high school math teacher asked him to write a treatise, which Norm knew the man wouldn't read, so Norm wrote only the first and last pages and shoved a pile of meaningless scratch paper in between; the time Norm's mother, who had been a watchmaker in the old country, quit her job as a seamstress sewing crotches for Hart, Schaffner & Marx, declaring, "I'm not a right crotch maker or a left crotch maker; I'm a *vatchmaker*!"; the time Norm was back from the service on medical leave with a cast on the leg he'd broken during judo practice, and a woman on the streetcar thanked him for all he was doing for his country, then asked if he'd been wounded in combat, and Norm said, "Ma'am, I don't like to talk about it." My father told more stories about Norm than about his own family.

I meet Norm at a Vagabond Inn on Colorado Boulevard in Pasadena, California, where he's been staying for the past week with his wife. He and Bess are here to attend dance performances choreographed by their granddaughter, who's getting a Ph.D. in astrophysics at Cal Tech. The rumor has always been that a genius gene runs through the Budow family.

Norm, who's wearing a striped rugby-style shirt with a white collar, a baseball cap, and blue jeans, looks shorter and frailer than I remember. He is just getting over two hip surgeries—one time he was hit by a car, another time by a mountain bike—and he had a heart attack on the operating table during one of these operations. Norm's wife, Bess, is suffering from macular degeneration and her sight seems to be deteriorating, an irreversible condition in her case.

"I'll have to picture you in my mind," Bess says as she greets me in their motel room, then tells me I remind her of my father.

"How so?" I ask.

"The warmth."

This is not a word I usually associate with my dad. But my father was always happy to see Bess and Norm, so I wonder if maybe she feels her own warmth being returned to her. Or maybe she just knows some aspects of my dad better than I did.

When I was a kid, Norm was always generous with hugs, handshakes, and backslaps, and sometimes when I saw him, I'd wonder how my life might have been different if he'd been my father. Even though they're now in their eighties, living in retirement in Santa Fe, New Mexico, they remain volunteers and activists, protesting a proposed nuclear waste site; lobbying for a living wage; volunteering once a week for the state agency for aging and disability; attending meetings of a Tikkun study group. Norm serves as vice president of Veterans for Peace in Santa Fe. Recently, he sang Pete Seeger's "Bring Them Home" with a Vietnam vet and a Desert Storm vet at Santa Fe Plaza. "You try to make a better place, a better world, a better country, and God knows we need it right now," Norm says. "People say they don't know what they want to do when they retire; for me, it's finding enough time to do everything I want."

Norm walks more slowly than he used to, and his face has gotten craggier. He walks with a limp as we make our way through the dry, blazing California heat (it's supposed to hit ninety-five today). *"Tempus fugit,"* he tells me. He says what he means by this is that his generation's disappearing; he points out that he's one of only two World War II veterans left in his antiwar group.

Norm seems to know more about the Bonus March than any of my father's other friends or relatives; he taught it at Truman College. "Oh yeah, it was a seminal event and it was a betrayal of our World War One troops," he says over breakfast in a Pasadena café. He rattles off the events, his speech fast, exuberant. "We were at the beginning of a depression and the government didn't wanna spend the money, so whaddaya do? You have mass action to get the government to honor what the government said it was gonna do, and there was a march on Washington. They set up the tent city at Anacostia Flats and, ironically, they called out the current troops to crush a march by World War One troops. It was not a shining light in American history."

Norm never talked about the Bonus March with my dad, though, and my dad never discussed the idea of writing a book about it with Norm. "I wish he had," Norm says. And as for my grandfather's involvement in World War I, Norm never heard about that, either; he only knew that Sam Langer was a pop man.

The Budow family moved from Russia to the States in 1923, two years before Norm and my dad were born, and Norm's earliest recollection of my father is of a boy across the hall walking with crutches. Though he says he was less of a "hell-raiser" than a "horser-arounder," Norm admits having been kind of a wild kid, but he says my dad was on the sidelines for most of his bad behavior. Norm accompanied my dad when he would go to the store to buy stamps for his collection. They would work together "dispatching" insects for science projects with cyanide eggs that Norm had procured via his family's photoengraving business. But when Norm would take books out of the library about explosives, go to chemical supply houses to buy pyrotechnical products, then make his own gunpowder and fire-crackers, my dad absented himself.

"It was a hazardous hobby," he says. "Your father was not involved."

Later in life, my father would pass along articles from *Commentary* or *National Review* for Norm to read, but Norm never thought much of them. Still, he says he didn't let my father's growing conservatism affect their friendship.

"Hell no, no way," Norm says. "But in my book, the neocons are kind of disgusting. And the irony of it is that the neocons were the architects of the Iraq war, and it's a double irony, because they themselves never put on a uniform. But during the Vietnam War, they sent off others and they supported it."

Still, Norm takes comfort in the fact that my father's conservatism seemed to wane and that toward the end of his life, he began to return to Norm's way of thinking. Shortly before he died, my father was at his kitchen table with Norm and asked, "Norman, do you think that the whole world is going to hell?"

"By the time he made that statement to me, it was readily apparent that these neocons were sludge, they had no integrity, and they led us down the garden path," Norm Budow says. " 'Has the whole world gone to hell?' your dad asked, and I had to say, 'Yes, I'm forced to agree.' "

1983

The house on Mozart Street is beginning to make me feel more and more claustrophobic. But I've finally got my learner's permit, and I'm going to be applying to colleges soon. I'm pretty sure that when I graduate from college, I'll work as a writer. I've already started writing a bit for neighborhood newspapers and working as a reporter and actor for two kids' radio shows on the local National Public Radio affiliate. I've had a letter to the editor published in the *Chicago Tribune*. I also recently entered a high school poetry competition with a poem about my addiction to cigarettes; the poem is entitled "I Am a Billboard." I've never smoked a cigarette, but I thought the topic would win me a prize, and I was right; my poem took first place.

In high school, I'm taking a journalism and English literature class, and our instructor, Mr. Reque, is one of the more exacting teachers I've had. The way he runs his class reminds me a little of Professor Kingsfield in *The Paper Chase*. Recently, upon the advice of my father, I wrote an essay for this class, wrongly contending that Ernest Hemingway's "Hills Like White Elephants" was about tuberculosis and not about an abortion. Reque gave my paper the C it deserved. I probably shouldn't still be relying on my father to help me with schoolwork; he tends to say everything's about tuberculosis even when it's not—it's one of my dad's two favorite topics: TB and the Bonus March.

I did better on a compare-and-contrast essay I wrote for Mr. Reque about the affinities between Jack Kerouac's *Dharma Bums* and George Orwell's *Down and Out in Paris and London,* which, my dad has claimed, argued the unavoidability of a lower class and the foolhardiness of trying to eradicate poverty. But the paper's not as insightful as my father seems to think. To my mortification, he submitted it to *Encounter,* one of his favorite magazines, cofounded by neocon forefather Irving Kristol. "Although we feel this is quite good for a school paper . . . ," the inevitable rejection letter began.

Mr. Reque has now assigned us to write college-application essays in which we will discuss a life-changing incident or one that reveals our character. In grading our essays, Reque won't give us just A's and B's, but also an "Accept" or "Reject."

I write an essay about a dispute I had with my father over

whether I would wear dress shoes or sneakers to a Chicago Symphony concert. The essay, in which my dad comes around to my way of thinking and lets me wear the sneakers, is, I feel, a humorous, lighthearted way of describing my persuasive talents while establishing my independence, my own mild-mannered form of teenage rebellion. I particularly like the respectful yet witty repartee in which my father and I engage in the essay. Mr. Reque seems to agree with me, because he writes "Accept" on the paper. The only problem with the essay is that nearly all of it is invented—the conflict, the dialogue, the resolution. I don't think my actual life is worth writing about; I have to add, invent, embellish. At this point in my life, I can't begin to think of any life-changing events I've experienced. If I feel angry with my father, I rarely have the heart or the courage to argue with him. I keep my thoughts to myself or write them down in stories that I type at a furious pace in my parents' basement while sneaking swigs of their liquor and blasting Elvis Costello. And whenever I go with my parents to the symphony, I always wear dress shoes.

LENNY

The more I talk to people who knew my dad as a young man, the more a different image of my father from the one I remember is beginning to emerge—more vulnerable and more human. He seems to have been a confidant, a faithful friend, a listener, a dreamer. I would have liked to know and understand that guy better. Even the tales he apparently invented or exaggerated show a different side of him, someone with whom I have more in common—someone less sure of himself, less confident of his own story, and therefore more inclined to make up stories the way I did in high school. The father I thought

I knew, the image that my father portrayed to me, would have finished his Bonus Army book in a matter of days—no rewrites, no edits. *Here it is; it's done. What's next? When's dinner?*

"Oh, your dad told me lots of stories," says Lenny Primer with a laugh when I mention the book my dad wanted to write. "You know what he used to tell me in high school? That he was related to Russian generals, that he was related to Timoshenko. You know what else? He told me his name used to be Sidney but he changed it to Seymour."

"Why did he say it was changed?"

"He said he changed it just because he didn't like the name Sidney."

"He told me a different story," I say. "He said he was sick and his parents had to change the name to fool the dybbuk."

"I don't remember him ever telling me that one," says Lenny, who laughs again. Apparently, Lenny thinks I'm gullible.

Some of my dad's friends moved out of town, some dropped out of sight, then reappeared later, some called only when they needed medical advice or to say that someone was in the hospital or had died, but Lenny was always there. In my father's last months, Lenny frequently called or came by. My father would say he didn't want visitors, but Lenny was different.

"To my knowledge, I was the closest person to him outside of his family," Lenny says as we sit on his couch in his Wilmette living room. "I was probably closer to him than his brother."

"Leonard talked to him all the time," says Lenny's wife, Sue, as she brings us two glasses of lemonade. "That was his buddy."

Lenny, who bears a striking resemblance in both physical appearance and manner of speech to the director, actor, and comedian Mike Nichols, was on the high school quiz team with my dad. They joined the band together, attended drawing classes at the Art Institute. They were near the top of their class at Marshall, one ranked number twelve, the other number nine, though Lenny says he can't remember who was which. Knowing Lenny, my guess is that he might well have had the higher rank but is being generous by saying he doesn't remember. Either way, every night when Lenny and my father would come back from school, they'd call each other on the phone.

"We talked all the time, like little girls," Lenny says. "I never did a thing without him and I'm not sure if he ever did a thing without me."

My dad and Lenny saw movies together, hung out in Garfield and Douglas Park, even bowled at the Cascade Bowling Alley.

"Can you believe your father used to go bowling?"

"No, I really can't."

"We went bowling and we never went out with girls," says Lenny. "We had a lot of girl friends, but we hardly went out with girls."

After high school, Lenny went off to the service. He says he was the kind of kid who was always drawing airplanes, so began as an aviation cadet. "They'd flash a picture of an airplane and it would be German or Japanese or American or English, and you had to tell which airplane it was, and I knew them all because I loved them." When Lenny was with the Combat Crew Training Unit near the Illinois-Indiana border, he'd visit my dad in college in Champaign. But Lenny didn't make it through pilot training, and he wound up going into radio school, then into the Troop Carrier Command.

"I could have just as easily gone into bomb-carrier command, where I would have been killed probably," Lenny says. "In the military, it's a flip of a coin whether you make it or not."

In 1945, Lenny was in Berlin with the Eighty-second Airborne Division. "My first night there, everything was loose," he says. "I had to carry a pistol like a cowboy and I couldn't find a place to sleep, so I found a clean toilet that hadn't been demolished and I put a door down and that's where I slept. Things were still tough; there was a curfew for the Germans and it was hot, and there weren't too many Americans, and I remember a plane landing that wasn't scheduled, and on the plane were Jack Benny and Ingrid Bergman. I still remember the first thing Jack Benny said: 'Would you ever believe me, Jack Benny, would be performing here in Berlin?' We went crazy. You know, when I look back, I realize I could write a book about me."

"Did you ever talk to my father about your service?" I ask. "Did he ever ask you about it?"

"No, I never did," says Lenny. "What would I have talked about? I don't think most people like to talk about their service. No, I don't think I did."

When Lenny returned, his friendship with my father became even stronger. And as Lenny tells stories of my dad, I begin to feel nostalgic for this father I never knew. Lenny says that he and his first wife, Bunny, were with my dad even on the night my brother was born. "He asked if we would come with him. He was so uptight about it that we went to the hospital with him. Here he was a doctor and he wanted us there."

When my dad ran into trouble during his first job out of med school as a general practitioner, Lenny was the one in whom he confided. "He wanted to get away from there all the time and we couldn't understand why. He finally said that he had been taking care of this woman, and some crazy guy came in and said, 'You've been molesting my wife.' And he hit your father. And your father said, 'That's bullshit and I'm not gonna take it,' and he quit. That's why he went into radiology. I guess I'm the only one who knows that."

When Lenny's first wife passed away, my father picked him up and took him for a ride in his car. "I was in bad shape," Lenny recalls, "and Seymour said, 'If I could do anything in the world for you, I'd do it.' But he couldn't do anything; nobody could."

My dad and Lenny often talked about projects on which they could work together. But though Lenny remembers the Bonus March ("MacArthur was the one who slapped them down. Patton led the troops. Eisenhower was on the staff. I was always a 'Quiz Kid' kind of guy; I know all this kind of stuff"), my dad never discussed the idea with him. Instead, he would talk about how the two of them could open a bookstore together.

"I used to laugh when he talked about it," Lenny says. "But who knows—if I would have gotten serious, maybe he would have gotten more serious."

Today, Lenny seems in decent health—lucid, youthful, vital, quick-witted, at least ten years younger than his eighty-three. But there's a price to be paid for outliving one's closest friends.

"I'm becoming a loner," Lenny tells me as we drink our lemonades. "Who knows what's gonna happen tomorrow?"

1984

I'm in my first semester of college in Poughkeepsie, New York, and I'm having kind of a rough time. This is the longest I've ever been away from Chicago. I have two roommates—one a rabid Van Halen and Night Ranger fan who blasts local hard rock station WPDH and is majoring in economics, the other a rabid Boy George and Vanity 6 fan who blasts New York's KISS FM and who is majoring in waking me up in the middle of the night to ask me personal questions, which are, unfortunately, outside my present knowledge base— for example, "What does getting teabagged feel like?" On my Roommate Preference Card, I probably shouldn't have written that I could get along with anybody.

My mother sends me letters every other day; my father doesn't write much, but occasionally he encloses a cartoon clipped out of *The New Yorker* or *Punch*. I've fallen in with an artsy, theatrical crowd, with whom I feel I have little in common—we go out for dinner, a group of about twelve of us every time, or we go thrift-shopping at the Salvation Army in downtown Poughkeepsie, but I usually come home early and run up large phone bills talking to my best friend, Paul, who's attending the U of I, then typing long letters to friends, playscripts, and college-application essays for the schools to which I'm considering transferring. When I finish one such essay, a bombastic screed about the closed-mindedness of the student body here, I call home to read it to my mother. But my dad answers the phone; he says my mom is out. And though I rarely reveal any more of my emotional state to my father than he does to me, I read the letter to him. After I finish, there's a long pause.

"It probably isn't that bad," my dad says, then tells me to wait before deciding to transfer. He then adds a piece of advice I've heard from him in multiple situations: "When in doubt, do nothing."

I decide to cheer myself up by taking a trip to Manhattan to see plays and go to museums. My father has given me five hundred dollars as spending money, which he says should last the whole semester, and I decide to spend a good chunk of it. I take the train down to Grand Central, catch a matinee of Tom Stoppard's *The Real Thing* and an evening performance of *Sunday in the Park with George,* then take the last train home, which gets me back to Poughkeepsie sometime after midnight.

But when I try to get into the Poughkeepsie train station, the doors are locked. And when I walk around to the front, only one cab is parked outside; by the time I get to it, it's already speeding away. The few people still here are getting into their cars and heading home. Soon I am alone in the dark in front of the locked train station.

Back in high school, I could always rely on my father to give me a ride home—that's one thing he truly liked doing outside of his job: answering the phone at any hour, going downstairs to his car, driving his black Ford. Now I'm living eight hundred miles away from home.

The pay phone outside is broken anyway—no way even to call a cab. My dorm must be three miles from here.

Downtown Poughkeepsie in the Reagan 1980s is a dismal place, a late-twentieth-century version of Depression-era America—shuttered and burned-out stores, homeless people sleeping on benches on the Main Mall, numbers runners plying their trade in shell businesses. I'm a sheltered teenager from the safe Jewish ghetto of Chicago—tired, afraid, walking with my hands in my pockets, eyes staring straight ahead, past the prostitutes loitering on street corners.

A few blocks into my walk, a stray black dog starts to follow me. For years, I've been afraid of dogs, so I walk more quickly. But the dog keeps pace. Soon he is walking beside me. I try not to pay attention, but there he is, trotting as I walk. I don't know which is more frightening—the vagrants milling about and gazing at the scared, preppy college kid or the dog at my side.

But soon I notice that people are beginning to get out of my way. They look to me, the easy mark, then to the dog, then back again, and they let me pass.

"Where's that dog's leash?" I hear them mutter. "Isn't it late to be out walking a dog?"

The dog is still walking beside me as I pass the Grand Union supermarket, the Big Tomato luncheonette, Two Brothers' Barbecue; all are closed for the night. Only when I reach the college gates do I stop, and there the dog stops, too. I move forward, but the dog goes no farther. I wait to see if he will come, but once I am on the other side of the gates, he turns and dashes back into town.

I am still alone, but I feel safe. Without anyone helping me, without my father to give me a ride home, I have found my own way. I am no longer afraid of dogs, but, perhaps even more important, I see that I can venture out into places where I don't feel at ease. And when I do, some of the stories I experience are better than the ones I can make up.

THE LEVINES

"No, I never knew he had a literary bent. He never mentioned it. Marlene, did you ever hear anything about Seymour wanting to write a book?"

"No, but he tiled the bathrooms in your house, Adam; he told me that once."

"We just never discussed politics. I don't even know if your father was liberal or conservative."

I'm in the kitchen of Seymour and Marlene Levine's house in the Budlong Woods neighborhood of Chicago. Marlene has made coffee and has set the table with bagels, cream cheese, muffins, and kolachkis; Seymour urges me to eat or drink. "Just take something," he says. "How 'bout a cup of coffee? A sweet roll? We got Muenster cheese."

This is hardly the first time I've been here. Though they went to high school and the U of I together, my dad and Sy Levine fell out of touch, but they got back together when I became friends with Seymour and Marlene's youngest son, Andrew.

Andy was in my tee-ball class at the JCC and was with me all through Hebrew school. He was a smart, funny redheaded kid who, as was the case with my father and some of his friends, was a bit wilder than I. Andy's string instrument was electric guitar, while mine was the violin. Andy pitched a tent in the backyard of his family's home and turned on the sprinklers to simulate a rainstorm; he knew how to tell someone to kiss his ass and go to hell in Hebrew, and did so in my family's basement; he got into trouble in Heh class for mocking the rabbi for following him to the bathroom—"You want to watch me go? Make sure I do it the kosher way?" One of the last times he came over to my house, Andy and I played Monopoly in my family's den with our Hebrew school classmate Amy Persky.

Later that day, Amy and I sat on the front stoop of my family's house while Andy rode his bike down the steps, then carried it back to the top, then rode it down again. Ultimately, Andy became the lawyer, while I became the writer. I was the one who married a deacon's daughter from southwest Germany; Andy was the one who married Amy; they have two kids now and a house in Skokie.

This morning, in the Levines' kitchen, I finally take a kolachki and a cup of coffee.

"Let me toast you a bagel," Marlene says.

Everyone else's family often looks so much more peaceful from a distance, but I always sensed that the Levines' house would have been a pleasant place to grow up: Sy Levine, the M.I.T.-educated engineer and attorney, with his measured manner of speaking; his wife, Marlene, who was in my aunt Donna's high school sorority and never seems to have a bad word to say about anybody. ("We love your mom's company; she's such a delight!")

I'm not sure if my parents ever had deep, soul-searching discussions with the Levines (or with anyone else, for that matter), but they liked going out with them. When I mention that some of my relatives didn't always appreciate my dad's caustic sense of humor, Sy and Marlene don't seem to recognize the person I'm talking about.

"We never had anything like that," says Sy.

"No, we never had that," Marlene says. "It was always a pleasant evening, and we went out quite a bit."

Sy met my father in high school. They didn't have classes or extracurricular activities together, though. Sy played clarinet in the band, which my father quit early on. Sy went to dances at the Jewish People's Institute, but my father didn't dance. Fifty years later, when I was going to school with Sy's son, not much had changed. At a Bar Mitzvah, I watched Seymour Levine dance with my mother while I sat with my dad. There was no more Bull Session, nobody lived on the West Side, and nobody went to the JPI, but the topics of conversation and the activities remained the same—my parents and the

Levines would attend concerts at Orchestra Hall, and then they'd talk about where they would eat.

"For many years, we used to get together with your folks and we'd go to Agostino's on New Year's Eve," Sy tells me. "We'd put on the hats and the New Year's Eve paraphernalia and celebrate. Your brother sent us a bottle of wine once, champagne. Apparently, they knew your brother there—he had a reputation. Your father told us all about it that night."

I remember that night, too. I remember it because I had sent over the bottle. I remember my mother telling me later how delicious the champagne had been and seeming puzzled when I told her that it was Asti Spumante. I remember thinking that sending a bottle of bubbly to my parents seemed like an uncharacteristically mature thing for me to do, and apparently my parents found it uncharacteristic, too, and assumed my brother had done it. Both my father and I imagined each other as people other than who we felt we really were.

"Actually, I was the one who sent the bottle that time," I say.

"Well, we're giving you your bonus now," Seymour Levine says. "We're paying you back with a cup of coffee."

1986

I drank too much Genesee cream ale my first year in college, but now that I'm a sophomore, I'm not drinking at all. I am involved in my first serious, long-term relationship, I've declared my major as political science, I work as the book editor of the college newspaper, and I am directing my first full-length play, a drama about a young woman named Katie, who is on her winter break from college and is still struggling to make the transition to adulthood. The play, which

I wrote in my parents' basement on winter break, is called *Almost Twenty*, and one of the characters is Katie's distant and disengaged father. Though I spent much of my time in high school with a crush on a girl named Katie, I'm still certain the show isn't remotely auto-biographical.

I've cast a guy named Ken as the father character, and he does a great job at the first few rehearsals—the character is funnier than I realized: smarter, more observant, less detached. But Ken has other commitments and ultimately has to drop out of the show, so I take the role. I wear the same cardigan Ken did, use some of his delivery style, play the role for laughs, try to see the foibles of his children from his perspective.

On opening night, my mom and brother come to Poughkeepsie to see the show. And after it is over, both tell me how convincing my performance was; up onstage, I acted so much like my dad.

GENE

"I'm still marching and I still haven't gotten a bonus," Gene Shalit tells me. "I march at NBC in front of the building every day. Still no bonus."

Shalit is the longtime arts critic for NBC's *Today* show, the man with the familiarly wild hair and bushy mustache. ("I paved the way for everyone who looks like a meshuggeneh on television," he says.) He has been spending his day decorating the screened-in porch of his New England home to make it look like a pirate ship, complete with a Jolly Roger, a steering wheel, and a gangplank. But he's taking time off to chat with me about his days at the U of I with my dad.

"It was a segregated town," says Shalit, who arrived in Champaign

Urbana in 1943. "Black students at the movie theater had to sit in the balcony. Steak 'n' Shake, like a lot of the sandwich shops in town, had a sign in the window that said, 'We reserve the right to seat our customers.' That meant black kids were not welcome. We had a protest and your father was part of it. We all went in at 11:00, before the rush, and we occupied every stool and table in the place and refused to move unless they let black kids in."

"What happened then?" I ask.

"What happened then? Nothing. The sign stayed in the window and that was the way it was," says Shalit. "But that was a different time, a different society. In those days, sororities were either all Gentile or all Jewish. The Gentile girls I knew couldn't go out with me, because if they dated a Jewish kid, they'd get fined five dollars."

During his first year in Champaign, Shalit says he lived with about nine other young Jewish men, including my father and Seymour Levine, in a house on 511 E. Daniel Street.

"Your father was a mensch," Shalit says. "He was everybody's friend if they had brains. Of all the people I lived with my first year, he is one of the only people whose name I remember. Two of the kids in our house were premed. One was your father. The other was a boy whose name I don't recall, but he was the antithesis of your dad. He was a kid who just studied, and he had a clock. He studied for fifty minutes, a bell rang, and he went on his bed and rested for ten minutes and then he started studying again. And I remember all of us saying, 'Someday, when you guys are doctors, we're all going to Seymour, because we don't want any part of this other guy; he is so rigid.' "

On the front lawn of the Daniel Street house, Shalit says, there was a building the size of a Pullman car, out of which a Jewish man sold hamburgers. The house itself was owned by a woman who took in students as boarders. The boarders didn't like the landlady, since she always told them to keep down their racket, so at night they would all gather in my dad's room to drop their shoes on the floor to wake her up. Once a week, my father and some of the other boarders would send their dirty laundry home to Chicago and their mothers would send back fresh laundry through the mail.

"I thought that was crazy," Shalit says. "I remember I was looked upon askance because I went to the Laundromat and paid the ten cents."

Shalit doesn't remember socializing much with my dad, other than going out to eat—a Chinese restaurant downtown charged seventy-five cents for a full dinner; the Quality Restaurant sold five-dollar tickets, which were usually good for a week's worth of meals. On Friday nights, they'd join other Jewish kids at a house on Springfield Avenue where a woman named Mrs. Seligman cooked Shabbos dinner.

Shalit says the time he spent in that house in Champaign with my father was the beginning of the most meaningful period of his life, one that paved the way for his entire career. But after my father graduated from the U of I and went to medical school, Shalit never laid eyes on him again. By 1949, Shalit was working for *Look* magazine in New York, and soon afterward, he would go into broadcasting. They still kept in touch, though, wrote each other letters. I remember my father writing one and feeling uncertain whether he could get it past Shalit's secretary, so he wrote "Check Enclosed" on the outside of the envelope; inside, he drew a check mark on a piece of paper. But even when Shalit was getting us tickets for Broadway shows, he and my dad never saw each other. And despite his nostalgia for college, Shalit returned only once to Champaign.

"I never go back," he says. "I know the elm trees died. I know they've built a thousand new buildings. I know they've got twenty-five thousand more kids than we had back then. But I never go back, because I want it to stay exactly as it was when I left in 1949. I want to preserve those years and that scene and that campus forever."

My dad wanted to write a book, I tell Shalit. Has he ever considered writing one?

·"Nah, I'm not gonna write my memoirs," Shalit says. "What am I gonna say in a book? Nobody cares about my life. I don't think anybody would be interested."

"But your memory seems so sharp."

"Well, maybe it would be nice to write something for my kids so they would know who their father was."

"Why? Haven't you told them these stories?"

"I'm very close to them. But I usually only ask them about what they're doing. I never really talk to them about any of this."

A few weeks after this conversation, I receive two letters. One is from the National Personnel Records Center in St. Louis, this time from a management analyst there. "I researched your request to determine if we have any WWI record for your grandfather," the analyst writes. "Unfortunately, we have no such record. It may be that his record was lost in the 1973 fire at this center, or it may be that he did not serve in the army."

The analyst has also enclosed copies of four ID cards of men from Long Island, Yonkers, Dubuque, and Cleveland. All of them served in the U.S. Army during World War I; all of them are named Samuel Langer; not one of them is my grandfather.

The other letter is from Gene Shalit, who has enclosed a copy of a letter my dad sent him in 1992 discussing their classmates. In the letter, my father mentions the house where Shalit has recalled living with him.

"About 511 Daniel," my dad wrote, "I did not live there."

"I'm startled and shaken by your father's assertion," Shalit writes to me. *"He didn't live there?"*

As I read my father's letter, which contradicts what Shalit told me before, I wonder how much I can trust any of these stories of the past I've been hearing, and how much I can trust my own memory, too. As Shalit writes in his letter's closing paragraph, *"Oy!"*

LOS ANGELES

I

It didn't take long for the members of the Bonus Army to tumble from fame to obscurity. Royal Robertson, the leader of the West Coast contingent of veterans, the bit-part Hollywood actor who led his "Death March" on the U.S. Capitol, collapsing twice on account of the heat and lack of sleep, returned to California shortly after the first bonus bill was defeated in Congress. Three years later, he was in Washington, D.C., petitioning the Roosevelt administration on behalf of needy California vets and threatening to lead another march. Less than three years after that, he died in a hospital in Hollywood at the age of forty-six.

Pelham Glassford, the D.C. police chief and one of the most sympathetic figures in the Bonus Army story, wound up in California, too. The brigadier general, who served under MacArthur and quit after the rout of the Bonus Army, died in 1959 in Laguna Beach, where he had become the head of a local arts festival and had attained a reputation as a watercolorist.

Up the coast in San Francisco, W. W. Waters, the commander of the Bonus Army, who made the cover of *Time* magazine in 1932 and was the coauthor of *B.E.F.: The Whole Story of the Bonus Army,* had become a "Where Are They Now?" story little more than a year later; he was working as an inspector on the San Francisco–Oakland Bay Bridge and living with his wife in a thirty-dollar-a-month apartment.

Today, on a flight from JFK to LAX, I sit next to a young woman named Carolyn, who is studying for her master's in social work at Columbia University. She is a trivia expert and knows quite a bit about the Bonus March; she is on her way to tape her second show on *Jeopardy!* after having beaten a five-time champ. She says she learned about the march in a history class.

"MacArthur, right?" she says.

I briefly fantasize about trying to learn how to become a game-show contestant, until Carolyn tells me ABC isn't picking up the bill for her night at the Radisson in Culver City.

I'll take Bonus March Trivia for 100, Alex.

Bonus March Trivia for 100: Best known for his novels and short stories, this manly author wrote an article for The Masses *entitled "Who Killed the Vets?"*

Who is Ernest Hemingway?

Yes!

Bonus March Trivia for 200, Alex.

Cartoon character Lisa Simpson complained she had kissed fewer boys than this Bonus March witness.

Who is Gore Vidal?

Correct.

Bonus Army Trivia for 300.

This Johnstown, Pennsylvania, Bonus Army encampment was once an amusement park but now serves as a Kidsport soccer field.

What is Ideal Park?

Yes!

Bonus Army Trivia for 400.

This Pennsylvania Republican-turned-Democrat said his decision to enter politics was influenced by the story of the Bonus Army.

Who is Senator Arlen Specter?

Correct!

Bonus Army Trivia for 500.

Closing out the category. And a Daily Double. This West Rogers Park physician spoke often to his youngest son of writing a book about the Bonus Army because his own father was a veteran of World War I.

Who was my father, Seymour Sidney Langer?

Ooh, I'm sorry. We haven't confirmed that World War I story yet. Anybody else?

"The Bonus Army was interesting," Carolyn tells me. "But I'm surprised that someone would want to write a whole book about it. Why do you think he wanted to?"

II

I'm seated at a long lacquered wooden table in the dim, windowless Special Collections Reading Room of the Charles E. Young Research Library of UCLA, where I'm paging through files in the Pelham Davis Glassford Papers, still searching for any hints about my father's story. The atmosphere is studious, the silence interrupted only by the rumble of the air conditioner and the occasional whirr of a pencil sharpener. Outside in the hallway is a silver shovel encased in glass, commemorating the groundbreaking for the building. The symbolism seems appropriate—I'm still digging. Behind me are bound volumes in locked glass-plated bookcases—Archimedes, Aristotle, Plutarch. Only two other researchers are here.

The Glassford Papers contain news clippings, files crammed full of them, scads of photographs, depositions, diary entries, the most material I've yet seen about the Bonus March. Which makes sense— if D.C. police chief "Happy" Glassford is remembered at all these days, it is for the role he played in the Bonus March. Plus, Glassford seemed to like seeing his name in print—it looks as though just about every article in which he was ever featured has been clipped and taped into his scrapbooks: "Glassford Made Kiwanis Member"; "Glassford Observes Marchers from Seat of New Motorcycle."

I've been wondering what the book my father wanted to write might have looked like. Glassford, for whom the Bonus March was arguably the central event of his professional life, never managed to succeed at writing a book about it, even with someone helping him. Here are outlines for a book, chapters, some in draft form, some written in collaboration with a member of the Bonus Army named L. W. Wade.

But any thought that Glassford himself could ever have penned a great Bonus March memoir quickly fades. The material here is one-sided—file after file of commendations for Glassford's comportment, editorials from newspapers, speaking highly of Glassford's treatment of veterans. The files suggest this man is not someone who wants to write a comprehensive history, but a man who is planning to appear before a committee and wants as much evidence as possible to back him up.

Glassford's chapter drafts seem cribbed from newspaper accounts; the writing relies on clichés. The most astute observations in these files come not from Glassford himself or his collaborator, but from a Welfare Commission observer named J. Prentice Murphy, whose dispassionate reports of the homeless people he encountered in the encampment in Johnstown, Pennsylvania, read almost like poetry:

- Father, mother, five children; mother pregnant; the youngest girl, a child, had convulsions the night before.
- A man a baker; lost his house in New York State; was evicted; he is going to his wife's relatives in Virginia.
- Man and wife and two children from Connecticut; lovely fine children; the baby is being breast-fed; going back to a relative.
- Man, wife, five children; long unemployment; desperately poor; man greatly discouraged; the little four year old daughter said she loved to have her mother read from a book about Jesus and the Lord.
- This family came from Baltimore; put on trucks at Washington; was not permitted to get off at a point near Baltimore; their baby has been sick in the Memorial Hospital, Johnstown; no plans.

As I work and read, gripped by these tragic true stories of then anonymous and now completely forgotten strangers, I wonder how different I really am from my father—the brainy, driven, fast-working kid with a limp, the kid with grandparents he never saw, relatives left behind in a land to which his father never returned and which he rarely discussed because he was too busy working. For my father and for me, a story about World War I may have felt like a way into that life, a way of trying to measure up to or make sense of it, a way of getting something—a story, the truth about where we came from—we felt our fathers owed us, a way, too, of giving to our fathers something that we felt they deserved.

Outside it's another glorious spring Los Angeles day, but I'm continuing to work in this basement, aided by artificial light. I'm not talking to anybody; I'm trying to understand a man by searching through the letters of strangers. I'm thumbing through files, scribbling notes on paper, examining photographs, putting them aside one after another: *This one I can use; this one I can't.* I'm beginning to understand what it feels like to be a radiologist.

1989

I'm about nine months out of college. I've broken up with my college girlfriend, I'm living at home, I'm driving a Ford Escort that my dad bought me from his cousins' Highland Park car dealership, and in my wallet I have the credit card my father gave me for emergency expenses, such as pants. I have scribbled three hundred pages of a diary in about two weeks. On one page I have written "I've gotta get outta here" nearly a dozen times. Recently, I had a dream that I was being held prisoner in my parents' house by the author E. L. Doctorow. Some of my dreams are hard to interpret; this one, not so much—my mother's initials are E.L. and my father's a doctor. It's time to move, but I haven't quite mustered the self-confidence to do it yet.

ADAM LANGER

My plan is to make as much money as I can in the next few months, then move out and get my first apartment. I've been working as a tour guide on a double-decker bus, as well as a Stanley Kaplan SAT test prep teacher in the Chicago public high schools. I've been writing freelance articles for Chicago alternative weeklies and magazines, and I've been acting in *Our Town*, *Romeo and Juliet*, and *A Midsummer Night's Dream* with the Arts Lanes theater company, which plays exclusively to high school classes and pays twenty-five bucks a show. The director is a retired Illinois State professor named Dr. Ralph Lane, who taught John Malkovich and other original members of the Steppenwolf Theatre Company. Dr. Lane is not particularly enamored of my acting in the role of Howie, the milkman, in *Our Town*. My performance, he says, reminds him of something he once told Malkovich: "People could be masturbating onstage right next to you and you wouldn't even notice." I'm too detached, Dr. Lane says, not emotionally involved in the action of the play.

I was casually dating a twenty-six-year-old social worker, but she stopped returning my calls after she figured out I was twenty-one and still living at home. I have a mild crush on an actress named Rachel Dratch, but she's not impressed with my living situation, either. "Cut those apron strings, Adam," she tells me. I was out on a date at a bar called the Vu with the heir to a chocolate-fudge fortune, who asked me if I was twenty-five. No, I told her, if I were twenty-five and doing what I'm doing, I'd be a loser.

At the family dinner table, I tell my parents that a few months from now I'll be moving out and getting my own place.

"I'd prefer you here," my father tells me. "I don't think I can afford to pay for your apartment."

"You probably could," I say, "but that's not the point."

A few days later, my father is upstairs at his desk, working on his taxes, and he tells me he has an idea. He suggests giving me "a couple thou" a month, which he can write off as a business expense.

"How would that work?"

"I'll say you're my chauffeur."

"No, thanks, Dad," I say.

I don't know if he's intentionally trying to belittle me or if he's just trying to inspire me to move on with my life, but that night, I make an appointment with the Apartment People.

| | |

Stories We Leave Behind

Americans never quit.

GEN. DOUGLAS MACARTHUR

My Father's Generation:
Scene from a Documentary

PART IIII: TWILIGHT OF THE BULL SESSION

By just about any measure, the members of my father's generation with whom I've been speaking have led successful lives. In their eighties now, they have seen their children grow up; they live in comfortable homes. Most of them are retired. Throughout their lives, they watched my father, monitored his progress, saw him become a doctor, a husband, a father, a grandfather, saw him lead a life much like their own. They still remember the kid they knew, the man he became; they feel his absence now that he is gone. Some of them still remember the Bonus March, but none of them seem to know what, if anything, it might mean: "Well, what are you doing about this Rosebud, Mr. Thompson?" "That Rosebud, that don't mean anything." I guess the Bonus March is just a piece in a jigsaw puzzle, a missing piece.

VOICES: **Irv Warso,** retired department store owner, Buffalo Grove, Illinois; **Howard Watt,** retired attorney, Phoenix, Arizona; **Sheldon**

Schoneberg, retired orthopedic surgeon, Woodland Hills, California; **Gene Shalit,** NBC television personality, New York, New York; **Ira Bell,** attorney, Wilmette, Illinois; **Lenny Primer,** retired advertising executive, Wilmette, Illinois; **Seymour Levine,** retired attorney and engineer, Chicago, Illinois; **Mitchell Schorow,** professor, New York, New York.

Irv Warso

(*Flipping through a copy of the 1943 Marshall High School yearbook*)

Here we go; let's see who we got here. Isaac Finfer, he lives in California.

(*Flips a page*)

Rosalind Sager, she lives in Joliet. She's pretty sick, I heard.

(*Flips a page*)

This is Putterman. Have you heard about Harry Putterman? He passed away.

(*Flips a page*)

This is Fox.

(*Flips a page*)

This is Orangutan Brown.

(*Flips a page*)

That's the guy in Arizona, Watt.

(*Flips a page*)

This guy here, he does something; I don't know what.

(*Flips a page*)

That's Michaelson; he died. His wife lives across the street.

(*Flips a page*)

This one died.

(*Flips a page*)

This one used to play a lot of golf, but not lately; I don't know what's going on. Her husband isn't well.

(*Flips a page*)

There's one of our guys; he passed away.

(*Flips a page*)

Nobody liked this guy. I didn't know him that well, but nobody liked him. He married a girl from the islands someplace and he moved down there. I think that's the guy; we sort of lost track of him.

(*Flips a page*)

This guy was in California and he died.

(*Flips a page*)

That's Sam; he died some years ago.

(*Flips a page*)

There is a guy somewhere in here, black fellow, by the way, Grisham. He became a big wheel on the South Side in the black community. He was in the papers quite a few times. I don't know if he's still around.

(*Flips a page*)

This guy, here, Friedman, became mayor of Northbrook; he's still around.

(*Flips a page*)

This guy lives in Paris. He worked for the government in France in some sort of capacity and he married some girl there and they bought some sort of residence and his wife died a couple years ago. He's still living there.

(*Flips a page*)

That's a friend of ours. He's very sick, I understand—dementia.

(*Flips a page*)

This guy had a heart attack or a stroke or something.

(*Flips a page*)

That's Al Zimmerman; he died.

(*Flips a page*)

This is Manny Barkin; he died. That was a sad deal. Who else we got here?

(*Flips a page*)

This guy wasn't in our class; he passed away.

(*Flips another page, pauses at a photograph*)

Oh look, here's your dad.

Howard Watt

When I got married, your dad and I were still in touch. My wife and I lived in an apartment hotel and we invited Sy and your mother over. That was over fifty years ago, but that's the last time I saw him. Both of us just sort of disappeared from each other's lives.

Sheldon Schoneberg

A few years back, I was in Chicago for our class's fiftieth reunion, and your folks had a dinner for me to meet all the old guys. I could recognize about ninety percent of them, but some of them looked so different. "Boy," I said, "there are a bunch of old men in this room."

Gene Shalit

I always thought your dad was a great guy, and I kept wishing I could get an X-ray so he could read it for me. Unfortunately, I was cursed by good health.

Ira Bell

When your dad died, I hadn't seen him in about seven years. I remember we were having a party, celebrating some good luck, and we invited your father, and he never even responded. I called him and he said no, he couldn't come. I said, "Well, you know, think about it." He said, "Well, it's too late anyway." I said, "It's not too late; the party hasn't happened yet. If you want to come, come." He never showed up. It's obvious that he was really just withdrawing. You could even tell it in our conversations—they became shorter. He was less verbal. You'd get more yeses and noes and less editorializing.

Lenny Primer

We'd call each other at least two or three times a week until he became very sick. Still, I'd go and visit. But that wasn't Seymour. We'd sit and talk and he'd doze off in the middle of a conversation. He'd just sit there and not say a word for half an hour. That wasn't Seymour.

SEYMOUR LEVINE

We could see the change in him. I think that many times, we were eating at Agostino's and he was in pain. Really. But the one thing you should know about him: He kept pushing and he didn't give up.

MITCHELL SCHOROW

When he died, I hadn't seen him in some time, I'm sorry to say. I wish I could help you out with that Bonus March he talked about, though. But you know what? God, I just wish you could meet my daughter. I think you could form a partnership. She would love to research something like that or work with you on that.

1991

I'm writing full-time now and I'm working in Chicago, mostly as a journalist but also as a playwright and theater producer. I've been dating a woman named Beate from southwest Germany, who came to work in Chicago during the Gulf War. On one of our first dates, she joined me for a theatrical protest against the war, during which I read a story about my kindergarten pal Beth Goldberg, who, in the story, is living in Israel while Scud missiles are being fired. Shortly after I told the story, I admitted to Beate that most of it was fiction. When I write, I still don't completely trust my own stories. I like starting with the truth, then veering away from it. But actually, I haven't seen Beth Goldberg since I was a kid; as far as I know, she doesn't live in Israel, either.

I'm now living in a bland, carpeted fourteenth-floor studio apartment on Oakdale Avenue. At $425 a month, the place is barely affordable, but the lake view makes it worth spending the extra forty bucks a month, which at first I wasn't sure I'd be able to earn. I love watching the lake, have loved it ever since I was a toddler going with my mother to Lunt Avenue Beach.

The other day, my father fainted in the parking lot of the U of I medical center and injured his knee. The knee's better, but while he was in the hospital, he contracted a staph infection, and now he'll have to stay there for another few days. I visited him the first day, and the only thing he really wanted to discuss was when he'd be able to "get the hell out of here."

I didn't visit him yesterday.

I'm at my typewriter table, trying to work on a play about my father, when I receive a phone call: my mother.

"You didn't visit yesterday," she says. "Are you going today? Your father misses you."

Later that day, on the way to West Rogers Park to pick up my mother, I stop at Radio Shack to buy batteries for my tape recorder. I hand my credit card to the man behind the counter, who takes a look at it, sees my last name, and asks if I'm related to Seymour.

"Yes," I say, "I'm his son."

"Your father was one hell of a ballplayer," the man says, and, when I ask, he tells me his name is Asher.

I can hardly imagine my father as any sort of athlete, but Asher is insistent and says no, he's not confusing my dad with my uncle Jerome. Seymour played catcher on the Marshall High playground, he insists, and he was a good hitter, too, and man, could he run the bases.

I pick up my mother and we drive to the hospital. I'm listening to Elvis Costello's *Spike* album, and as we pull into the parking lot, the song "God's Comic" begins to play. "Now I'm dead, now I'm dead, now I'm dead," Costello sings.

"*Oy*, what an awful song," my mother says. "Why are you listening to that? 'Now I'm dead, now I'm dead, now I'm dead'? What a terrible song."

When we get to the hospital room, my father is still talking about when he'll get the hell out of here. To change the subject, I tell my father about Asher. Yeah, my father says, he remembers Asher.

But is the story true? I ask my dad. Did he used to play baseball? Did he play catcher at Marshall?

"That guy must be senile," says my father.

INDIANAPOLIS

Lately, I've been getting up early every morning and driving from Bloomington, Indiana, to eerily empty downtown Indianapolis to research the Bonus Army at the national headquarters of the American Legion. During the first and second marches, veterans from Chicago would pass through the Hoosier State, holing up in the Salvation Army in Hammond, spending nights in parks in such towns as Roby and Seymour, Indiana, before heading out to Cincinnati, ultimately bound for Washington. But in this state, the closest item I've found to a public acknowledgment of the disenfranchised World War I veterans' plight is a statue of an anonymous doughboy in Spencer, Indiana.

I've been thinking a lot about the Bonus March during the daytime, but when I go to sleep, I usually start thinking about my dad. Each morning before I've headed out to Legion headquarters, my alarm has awakened me from an all-too-vivid dream about him. It's happened six nights in a row.

In the first dream, I was seated with my parents in the Lincoln Village Theater, watching the movie *Flashdance*. I never saw this film with my father, but it came out around the time when I was too young to drive a car and my dad would still go with me and my mom to movies—often, we wound up seeing something I was embarrassed to watch with my folks (for example, *An Officer and a Gentleman*). In my dream, *Flashdance* had been going on for some time, but as it continued to play, some people started dragging a gurney down the aisle, then out a back exit. Somebody had died, and a stench had begun to permeate the theater, so much so that little by little, everybody started walking out.

In the next dream, I was in the passenger seat of my father's black Ford. Most of the times I dream about my father, he's driving a car, and he drives the way I always remember him driving, not fast so much as impatient, one foot on each pedal—*accelerator, brake, accelerator, brake.* We were heading south on Asbury Avenue toward Howard Street—the Evanston-Chicago border. I told my dad that he needed to speed up because we were going the wrong way and I was already late for a presentation I had to deliver for history class—in my neurotic dreams, I'm always late for a test or to turn in a paper, and the subject is always history. My dad sped up and pulled into a 360-degree turn and we almost got hit by an oncoming car. Then he continued driving in the same direction he had been going before the turn.

In the next night's dream, I was at my father's bedside in the hospital and he told me that one of our cousins had had a series of strokes, four of them. I asked my father how bad they were and whether our cousin might recover. "It's worse than mine," he said.

Yesterday, I dreamed that I was naked in the backseat of my father's car and he was driving fast off Lake Shore Drive onto a path of mud and grass. I had been discussing Nikola Tesla in the car with my brother, but when I saw us going off the road, I started shouting to my father that we would crash. My brother told me everything would be okay, after which I started repeating a mantra to myself: "Onions, onions, onions, and soup. Onions, onions, onions, and soup."

In this morning's dream, I was in my father's car, and once again he was driving. I was in the backseat beside my sister, talking about the Bonus March and the fact that my father never finished the book he wanted to write about it. I asked her why she thought he never wrote it.

"Because he ran out of time," she said.

At the American Legion headquarters, I've been working at the desk of the Legion's national historian. After the marchers had been kicked out of Washington and Johnstown and had either gone back home or started to drift around the country, the Legion was one of those places where you could actually witness the tide of national opinion turning in favor of the veterans in their quest for the bonus. Before the march, in 1931 at the Legion's national convention in Detroit, the membership's vote was nearly two to one against having the government pay the bonus. But after Douglas MacArthur's show of force embarrassed so many Legion members, at the 1932 national convention in Portland, the vote was overwhelmingly in favor of immediate payment.

I have been studying the minutes of the 1932 meetings at the Legion's annual convention, as well as piles of books, plus issues of the *American Legion Monthly.* But I don't feel as if I'm learning much more about my father or his relationship to the Bonus March, about why he was interested in the story or why he told it the way he did; nor do I feel any closer to him. It is not just that the men in the framed pictures on the walls here between the archives and the executive committee meeting room bear no resemblance whatsoever to any of his friends, relatives, or colleagues, not only that I cannot begin to imagine him in the company of any of the middle-American white males in these photos. It is not only that he would have had difficulty sitting in a car or a plane for the drive or flight to Indianapolis but also that I cannot imagine him here doing what I'm doing. I can imagine him reading X-rays in a room like this, sure, perhaps more so if the room were darker, but not scrolling through this microfilm, not sifting through these files. In this morning's dream, my sister said the reason he didn't write the book was that he'd run out of time, but today, I'm wondering if he would have written it even if he had all the time he needed.

Here at the American Legion, I'm having trouble imagining my father, who labored over drafts of the brief letters he wrote to the editors of medical journals, writing hundreds of pages of history. I can't imagine the man who frequently avoided conversations with his neighbors and his in-laws conducting interviews with witnesses or descendants of the Bonus Army marchers whom he sought with his *New York Times Book Review* queries. I can't imagine the man who never took a trip that lasted more than three days driving here. I can't imagine him among all these goyim. I can't imagine him in Indiana. I can't imagine him in this library. I can't imagine him in any library—did he ever go with me to the library? No, he'd drop me off at the Skokie Public Library, where I'd study, take out books with my uncle Jerome's library card, then wait for my dad to pick me up.

After my last day of research at the Legion, I take a detour on my drive back to Bloomington, stopping at Shapiro's Delicatessen and Cafeteria on South Meridien Street. The deli has been in business since 1905, and as I enter and smell the herring, chicken soup, bagels, corned beef, and pastrami, I am reminded of delis where I used to eat with my dad and the rest of the family—the Pickle Barrel on Howard Street, Ashkenaz on Morse Avenue, the Bagel on Devon, Sam and Hy's in Skokie. Here in the cafeteria line as I order a chopped liver and onion sandwich on rye bread with a bowl of matzoh ball soup, I feel for the first time since I've been in Indiana that I'm someplace where my father would actually have gone; in a deli, not in a library or a microfilm reading room, I finally feel like my father's son.

I sit at a window table with my sandwich and soup and gaze out the window.

"Onions, onions, onions, and soup," I say to myself. "Onions, onions, onions, and soup."

1992

Beate and I have been in a relationship for more than a year, and un-like some of the women I'd been seeing (most of them conflicted ac-tresses), she seems, to me, to be something of a badass—refused to take part in a church confirmation ritual when she was fourteen; marched down to the civil registry in Offenburg, Germany, to resign officially from the Protestant church; took a two-hundred-mile solo bike ride at age fifteen to visit one of her high school teachers, with whom she watched Pink Floyd's *The Wall;* left her parents' home when she was seventeen; supported herself by working as a telephone operator and got in trouble when she told a threatening caller to kiss her ass; scandalized her parents by summering in La Rochelle on the French Atlantic coast with her female phys ed teacher; came to Chicago to work for a Jewish organization as part of a German pro-gram performing acts of atonement for the Holocaust; blew off one of our first dates because she was protesting the Gulf War.

Lucky for me, my Jewish upbringing and my writing career make me something of a novelty to her. Beate has moved into my tiny apartment, and save for the few times when I make impolitic re-marks (such as asking whether she thinks dating me is serving the cause of German-Jewish relations), we rarely argue. If my parents have any problem with the fact that I'm living with a woman from Germany, they've never said so.

Beate and I spend nearly all our free time together—she tries to teach me German and quizzes me about the myth of the American Dream; I have tried to come up with original exercises to improve her already-pretty-good English pronunciation (for example, "The nude dude was rude when he glued his spoo to the food"). I have also informed her that, despite what the word may connote in German, calling my writing "grotesque" is not a compliment.

This weekend, I have an assignment for a local magazine to visit the Wisconsin Dells and interview and photograph Tommy Bartlett, founder of the legendary Tommy Bartlett waterskiing thrill show. Before we attend the show, Beate and I dine at Chuck E. Cheese's, then return to our dingy motel room, where Bartlett has sent us a bottle of cheap champagne.

In the room, Beate and I discuss the concept of heroes, a topic that she seems to find typically American—because of their history, Germans are leery of hero worship, she says, and the only individuals she can even begin to see as role models are Rosa Luxemburg, Doris Lessing, and Simone de Beauvoir. As for me, I tell Beate that I've always had heroes—when I was five and wanted to be a ballet dancer, it was Edward Villella; when I wanted to play for the White Sox, it was Richie Allen; in high school, I idolized Woody Allen and Jack Kerouac; in college, Bob Dylan, Ray Davies, and Stephen Sondheim.

But now, when Beate asks who my heroes are, I come up with an answer that hadn't occurred to me before: my parents. I begin to think about how closely their life stories hew to the myth of the American Dream that Beate and I have been discussing: my mother, who spent some of her childhood growing up in the back of a store on the old West Side; my father, son of a veteran and a soda-pop trucker. I think of their journeys from the West Side to West Rogers Park. So I tell Beate that right now, my heroes are my mom and my dad. I worry that she will think my remarks are corny or disingenuous, but luckily I am still exotically American and she says she finds what I have said naïvely charming. We open the bottle, regretting that we are in the Wisconsin Dells and not on the French Atlantic coast, where the champagne would be better.

BELLA

"Have you talked to Millicent?" Bella Stein asks. "She'd know more about your father than me."

Bella hasn't seen or spoken to many of her old friends lately. She lives in a gated community in Northbrook, Illinois, and she's awaiting treatment for an acute health condition. Her breathing is labored.

"It's a new ball game now," she says.

Back when she knew my dad, though, Bella was an athlete, a volleyball player, daughter of a tailor and a homemaker on Jackson Boulevard, just a few blocks west of my mom's family. She says she was one of the few women who hung out with my dad's crew.

Bella remembers spending time with my dad and the rest of the Bull Session members at their classmates' houses, eating chips and pretzels, playing games like telephone. Her one vivid memory of the time she spent with the group was turning off the lights in Bernie Singer's home to tell ghost stories, but then Bernie's parents came home, to find a group of teenagers with the lights out in the bedroom, and they got the wrong impression.

"We didn't think about sex or anything; we just thought about having fun," she says. "Can you believe that?"

"You should talk to Millicent," she says again. "Your father had a crush on Millicent."

"Do you have any other memories of my father?" I ask.

"No, I just know he had a crush on Millicent."

"Did she have a crush on him?"

"I don't think that way. I think she thought of him more as a friend."

"Well, things turned out okay for him anyway, I think," I say.

"Oh, I'm very fond of your mother," Bella says. "Is she still in the home? Is she still in there?"

"Yes," I say. "She's been in that house since about 1960."

"Good for her," Bella Stein says, and takes a breath. "Good for her."

1995

Now journeying back and forth between Chicago and Ithaca, New York, where Beate is in graduate school for political science, I am still nostalgic for my parents' West Side past. For my father's seventieth birthday, I write a play that extrapolates on the few stories he told me of his childhood. Titled *The Pop Factory*, with an all-too-intentional play on the word *Pop*, it tells of double-dealings, romances, and the vagaries of business from the perspective of a slightly disabled boy who works at the factory. It even features an original 1930s-style song, "Pop Bottle Blues" ("She seemed so very bubbly / But I feel flat just the same / Can I get back my deposit / On my pop bottle dame . . ."). I intend the play as a tribute to my father's youth, which I still manage to perceive as idyllic.

After I finish the script, I immediately drive it over to my dad, who whips through it in little more than an hour. When he's done and I ask what he thinks, he tells me I've actually gotten most of the details wrong—people didn't swear at the factory like my characters do, no one bantered about women the way they do in my play, and as for the song, he doesn't "get it."

Clearly, I don't know as much as I thought I did about my father's life. I've guessed at it and have gotten it wrong, but the truth is that I kind of like the way I've imagined it. I put the play in a drawer; I need to start trusting my voice and get back to working on stories of my own.

MILLICENT

In a video I shot of my parents in their home in 2000 shortly before I moved out of Chicago, my father is sitting at the head of the kitchen table in an armchair and my mother is paging through flower catalogs as she considers whether she'll plant daphne in her front yard. I'll be moving to New York soon for an arts-journalism fellowship at Columbia University, and I've come over to the house to show my parents the new video camera I purchased for the road trip Beate and I will take there. I'm training the camera on my dad, then my mother, then my dad again. They both look tired. I've been feeling tired and a little bit sick, too.

My father has just gotten off the phone with Millicent Marks, an actress with whom he attended high school, and he's nursing a glass of scotch. Millicent asked if he wanted to accompany her to visit a friend in Buffalo Grove. He said no. My conversations with my dad have often been clipped—brief exchanges, a pause, another brief exchange, silence—but lately they're even more so.

"I didn't want to go out there," he says.

"To Buffalo Grove?"

"Yeah."

"Why would you?"

"I wouldn't."

During my father's life, I never met Millicent Marks, but during the last times I saw him, he often talked about her. Had Millicent called? he'd ask. Maybe he should call Millicent. Millicent called when my mother had been out; did he mention that Millicent had called? I could never tell if she was his first true love or just one of several roads not taken. When I was a kid, the nostalgic way my father spoke of Millicent made me vaguely uneasy, the same feeling I still get now when I hear my father described by a high school pal as "a great lover" or some such thing.

"I remember when she called me after her husband died," my father says of Millicent as I watch him through my video camera's viewfinder.

"When was that?" I ask.

"About ten years ago," my dad says. " 'Charlie died. He never made a living.' That's what she said."

"What did he do?"

"Originally, he was a lifeguard," my father says.

My mother looks up from her plant catalog.

"Who are you talking about?" she asks.

"Millicent's boyfriend," I say.

"Husband," my father says, correcting me. "Originally, he was a lifeguard and then he worked as a cabdriver."

"And remind me—what was her claim to fame?" my mother asks.

"She was an actress at the Goodman," my father says, and takes another drink of scotch. "Her roommate was Geraldine Page."

"A long time ago, I heard that," says my mother.

My father takes another pull of scotch.

"That's a strong drink," he says.

Millicent lives in Beverly Hills now, has ever since 1947, when she married Charles Marks, who was, she says, a men's clothing salesman, not a lifeguard or cabdriver as my father had claimed. But back when she knew my dad on the West Side, Millicent was the spunky and theatrical daughter of a ladies' handbag manufacturer, living on South Spaulding Avenue, where a hospital parking lot now stands. Today, she's still working in L.A.—as a speech-language therapist and an English as a Second Language teacher at a Yeshiva. When I first spoke to her over the phone, she told me she would call me "Adam." My father was the only "Langer."

When I meet Millicent at her home, I wait for her to tell me how much I do or don't look like my father. She has never met me, and I'm curious about what she'll say. I wonder how I'll react if she tells me that I look just like him, or that I don't resemble him at all. But, though she smiles and hugs me upon my arrival, she seems to look past me.

"Do you favor your mother or father?" she asks. She has a sturdy and forceful presence as she stands before me wearing a pale green sweater and pearls. But she is still not looking directly at me, and I quickly realize that she has all but lost her sight. She's the third person I've met from my father's generation who is suffering from macular degeneration. Millicent has only her peripheral vision now. "I can just see that you wear glasses," she says.

We enter her house, where she has finished making roast chicken for Shabbos dinner, and sit in her living room on a couch with a floral pattern on it. "It was a silent love affair from far away and very close. And it was very wholesome indeed," Millicent recalls of her relationship with my dad.

No chance of mistaking Millicent Marks for my mother—where my mother can be reserved, Millicent is effusive, her voice trained for the stage; while my mother is prone to understatement and subtext, Millicent is given to bold, dramatic pronouncements. "Very flamboyant, very exuberant" is how she describes herself. "If I want to hug you, I will hug you, I don't care who's there. If I feel like I have to tell you something right now and I need your attention, I will demand it." And if Millicent is the near opposite of my mom, she is the complete opposite of my dad, seeming to display more emotion in a single conversation than he did in a lifetime of short conversations I had with him.

No, my dad never discussed writing the Bonus March book with Millicent. She says she doesn't recall the march at all. But when I tell her about it, she says that "Langer's" interest in it makes sense.

"Langer certainly always stood up for the underdog or for the one who he thought was mistreated in some way," she says, citing the example of Tommy Hill, a black teen who attended Marshall High with them. According to Millicent, Tommy was picked on by their classmates, who called him "Ol' Dummy Tommy." Tommy did poorly in school because he didn't try, and spent most of his classes drumming on his desk. He didn't even have his own locker at the high school.

"I said, 'Tommy, why can't you share my locker with me?' " Millicent recalls. "And Langer was very very proud of me. He said, 'You're the only one who would stand up for him.' He was very much for what was right, for righteousness."

Millicent Marks was Millicent Zadowsky when she knew my father, and she lived with her parents and her grandfather, who was religious, so she couldn't go out with my dad until after sundown on Saturday nights. Then they'd take the streetcar or catch a cab to a show or a party at a friend's house. Sometimes they'd go to the home of Bernie Singer, she says, sometimes to one of the girls' houses. But wherever they would wind up, the kids would talk and laugh and play spin the bottle.

"Oh, that was the highlight of our evening," says Millicent. "If the bottle would land on me, I would take Langer and we'd go back into the bedroom and we'd make the loudest smacking noises you ever heard, and if it landed on him, he would take me back there and, oh, *smack smack smack* again. We came out with big smiles on our faces, oh, all the jolly things that young foolish kids do; we had such fun."

My father couldn't dance well, but sometimes he would ask Millicent to dance anyway. "He couldn't keep time, and yet we kept time in our own way," she says. "We kept our own beat. He wanted me to have all the experiences like all the other kids. We would just hold hands and keep rhythm to the music. He wanted to partake of everything so that I shouldn't be denied. He was very unselfish, the most unselfish person. At least toward me."

Millicent says my dad was popular in her family's home. He'd chat with her sister or debate military strategy with her dad, who was something of an amateur historian. "They were proud of him somehow," she says.

Millicent studied acting at the Goodman Theatre, which she attended with the comedian Shelley Berman and where, as my dad said, she roomed with Geraldine Page (Millicent calls her "Gerry"), and my father was one of Millicent's biggest fans. He'd go to her opening nights with a bouquet of flowers. She'd practice monologues for him; they'd see shows, dissect them afterward. "He was very, very critical and some of his criticisms were very stinging and very good. He came right to the point.

"He always had his favorite seat on the aisle," Millicent says, "and I didn't let him come up to the dressing room because the stairs were very windy. I always came down. It was very, very lovely. It was just a very beautiful relationship that we had together. He was really such a wonderful young person."

Millicent didn't know what sorts of jobs my father had during the summers when he was going to college, but he always seemed to have money—whenever they would go out, he would treat. "One time, he even gave blood and got some money for it," she says. "We were going to the Drake Hotel, and I don't know if it was my birthday or what, but I said, 'Langer, how did you get all this money?' And he said, 'Oh, I gave some blood.' And I said, 'What do you mean you gave your blood?' And he said, 'They needed blood, so I gave my blood and I got paid for it.' And I just said, 'Oh, okay, this really is blood money.' "

Millicent went to New York to pursue an acting career, taking classes and working as a hatcheck girl until she got married and moved west. But if she hadn't left Chicago, she wonders if she might have married my dad.

"It's just that I had gone to New York," she tells me, "but otherwise, I do believe that we might have married."

When Millicent was married to Charlie and my father was married to my mother, Millicent says that she and my dad would continue to talk, but when they would see each other, the dynamic had changed. She could no longer be as effusive.

"A few times when we all went out to dinner, it was altogether under different circumstances," she says. "I realized our positions. Until then, I don't think I did realize our positions."

They still talked on the phone, though. My father would call Millicent to see if she was coming to town for this or that reunion, and when she would say no, he'd ask if she needed money and wanted him to buy her a plane ticket ("No, Langer, I don't need any money," she'd say). The last time Millicent saw my father, she says, he was wearing a neck brace and sitting in a wheelchair. My father liked having control of situations, and he didn't enjoy socializing when he was feeling ill, but Millicent insisted on visiting.

"I said, 'I don't care what you want me to do.' Though he was very opinionated and very strong-willed, maybe I was just a bit more than he. I went over. Of course I did; there was no doubt about it—that I should be in Chicago and I'm not going to see him? It was crazy. And, of course, I can't see very well anymore, and so I told him, 'Look, Langer, as far as I'm concerned, you are exactly as I left you before I got married. To me, you'll always be my Langer, so I'll come and see you, because I'm not *seeing* you.' And when I put it that way, he seemed very comfortable.

"I've lost a child, my oldest daughter. I have lost my parents, I have gone through tragedies," Millicent Marks tells me. "But when Seymour left, I felt my whole youth was gone, because he knew me then."

When I leave Millicent's house, she follows me out onto her landing. Though she can't see the blooming magnolia tree on her block, she can still smell it. As we stand together, she breathes it in.

"Isn't it lovely?" she asks.

2002

Two days before my father's seventy-seventh birthday, a few months before my parents' fiftieth wedding anniversary, and about half a year before my dad will finally retire, he is staying at home by himself while I'm in town, taking my mom to the ballet. Though my dad still works every weekday, he rarely goes out anywhere else. His high school friends will call to make plans, but he frequently will cancel at the last minute. Even a trip to Myron & Phil's seems like a chore, despite the fact that it's just a five-minute drive away. We've been talking about his having hip-replacement surgery, but it's risky, especially at his age. A boorish orthopedic surgeon saw my dad, and when my mother asked about the dangers, the doctor said, "He could wind up dead."

Tonight, I have asked my mother to use my video camera to shoot our route from West Rogers Park to Lake Shore Drive so I can remember it when I'm back in New York, where I've begun work on a novel that takes place in my old neighborhood. My mom and I have always been able to discuss just about anything, but she doesn't like bringing up unpleasant matters, and so, though she's clearly thinking intensely about my father's health, instead of talking about it, she's doing a lot of what I refer to as "blowing air." She takes a deep breath, holds it, lets it out. And then she does it again. When we're not talking about books or movies, our conversations tend to go like this:

(Breath)

"Mom?"

"It's just . . . nothing."

"What were you going to say?"

(Breath)

"Ma?"

"Forget it. Let it go."

"What?"

"Let it go, let it go."

Tonight, as we pause at a stoplight near Hollywood and Ridge, my mother lets out a breath.

"Mom?"

(Breath)

"Ma, what?"

"Well, I just don't know about your dad going in for surgery," she finally says. "I know people do it, and they turn out all right, but he has so many things wrong with him. 'Cause he's let it go for so long. Now it's two hips and two knees."

"Yeah," I say, "but there has to be an alternative to sitting in a chair, unable to move the whole time he's home."

"I know," says my mother. "I know that. I just don't know, though. He's let things go, but that's his nature from way back—nobody do anything about anybody, even himself or you or anybody. 'Just let it go; it'll be okay.' "

"Generally, it's worked out okay, but after a while . . . ," I begin. Then I let the thought go and add, "If he would just agree to do something, if he would agree to try a wheelchair out—"

"No, he won't," my mother says. "I brought up a walker from the basement. I thought maybe there would be less strain on his hands, I thought it would be easier, but he said no, so I'll bring it back down. I brought him another cane, a four-pronger; he didn't want that, either. It seemed a little wobbly, so I was going to have it fixed. He said no. I understand; it's a big deal for him."

"I understand, too, Ma," I say, getting more frustrated, "but he can't just sit in one place and do nothing when he's home. It would be one thing if he'd read a book."

"Or draw," my mother says. "Or read the paper for more than two minutes. Or write."

"Yes, or finally write his book," I say. "He can still do it. But at this point, just about anything would be a step in the right direction."

"I really don't know," my mom says. "He's done whatever he wants all these years and I can't tell him what to do. I don't even know what to do."

She points the camera out the window as we approach Lake Shore Drive. Once again, her speech is subdued, while her words are full of grim portents.

"What's going on out there?" she asks as she points the camera at an ambulance driving the other way. "See, there's a flashing red light."

MARTIN GORBIEN

I'm in the office of the chairman of the geriatrics division of Rush University Medical School. A gerontologist has to be something of a jack-of-all-trades—part general practitioner, part psychiatrist, part caseworker. Other than his dentist cousin, Lou Bulmash, my father saw few doctors in his life and, when it became necessary to do so, Martin Gorbien was summoned. My mother never seemed to like how the doctor treated her husband, not giving appropriate respect to his position, his accomplishments—"Like he's talkin' to nobody," she'd say. But in talking to Gorbien, I hope to discover if, as an outsider and a fellow physician, he might have a better perspective on my father's life—what he accomplished, what he left unfinished, and what seemed most important to him in the end.

"Your dad's case was presented as many cases in my practice are," Gorbien says, "that things are just kind of a mess without a concrete name, such as a fever or a broken bone or a heart attack. There's a lot about your dad that I remember very well. He had just retired and he was so frail and so immobile and so riddled with arthritis and congenital problems. Part of our mission was to find out what was new and what was old and what was different about his immobility and his declining function. And it struck me at the very first visit that he had some degree of cognitive impairment and it struck me, too, that he had still been working. Because if I had met him and I hadn't been given any history, and someone asked, 'Has this person been working?' I would have said, 'I really doubt it.' When I learned that he had been driving himself from Rogers Park to the University of Illinois, getting out of the car, getting by on crutches and canes, I was struck by his tenacity, his determination. It really was incredible."

"After fifty years of working, does a certain amount of routine kick in," I ask, "so that he might have been able to do his job almost by instinct?"

"Especially for someone who was as bright as your father was, there is a lot of routine," Gorbien says. "It was always described to me as his career being the center of his life, that he loved his career and it had so much meaning for him. It wasn't until much later that I learned that he liked to draw and that he was a very good artist. Obviously, he was very determined, but part of the reason why I might not have as much to say about him as I would with someone whom I spent equal amounts of time with or less, is that your father didn't talk to me very much. Even when given opportunities to really cut loose and tell me what was on his mind, he had very little to say. Over the time that I knew him, he became more withdrawn. Granted, he was very sick, but he was never much of a talker with me. His answers were always simple and there were never any wasted words—'I'm fine' or 'I'm not fine.' Most of the time, he said he was fine. He didn't complain about pain in situations where one might have assumed that he had pain."

"He never seemed to be one to talk too much about what was going on inside his head," I say.

"From a physical standpoint, he minimized everything," says Gorbien. "Here was this man who hadn't seen a doctor in thirty or more years. I can't emphasize enough how startling it was to see him in the condition he was in and the irony of him being a physician. Of course, this was not the first time that a physician hasn't jumped all over getting care for himself. But every joint in his body—knees, hips, back—was so deformed. Many of his joints were almost completely fused and we had to try to unravel the story of what could be fixed. His response to his own situation was the opposite of mine: 'What's everybody so excited about? This is how I am.' "

My brother and I had a talk shortly after my father died, I tell Gorbien, and I said it seemed to me as if my father had made a bargain that he would live without confronting his physical problems and would be able to function for a very long time, but not forever. And for that, he would pay a very large price in the last few years of his life, but it was one he might have been willing to pay. "One thing I didn't know before I started talking to people," I tell Gorbien, "was that he spent a lot of his childhood on and off crutches and in and out of hospitals."

"Yes," Gorbien says, "he was someone who had had those childhood experiences that, to some degree, colored his decisions as to how he cared for or neglected himself, and he became a doctor in a specialty where he took pictures of everyone else's bones and joints as he walked around with his own bones and joints that were so distorted."

"When you speak of cognitive impairment, is that something you saw growing over time?" I ask.

"Yes," says Gorbien. "He was quiet, though, and sometimes people are quiet because they don't want to make a mistake; they don't want to speak up, for fear of embarrassing themselves. So there's a social awareness that prevents people from misspeaking. But your father had areas of memory that stayed intact for quite some time. Even up to the very end, there were areas where he was very, very sharp. Even at a time when he was almost nonverbal and he was so withdrawn, he would come out with a zinger and say something that was right on target."

"Was dementia something you noticed when you first saw him?"

"The theory was that your father had vascular dementia, the second most common form of dementia," Gorbien says.

"And how does that manifest itself differently from Alzheimer's?"

"They're very similar, but there are subtle differences early on.

Alzheimer's tends to decline over time, whereas vascular dementia is described as a stair-step decline."

"And those are both irreversible paths?"

"Vascular dementia, if you treat the underlying problems, such as hypertension or diabetes, can be slowed," says Gorbien, "whereas with Alzheimer's, we have less to modify. But in terms of how the person looks and behaves, there are more similarities than differences."

"And in terms of memory loss, is there any kind of rule? What is remembered? And what is forgotten? My dad could draw from memory the factory where he and his father worked, but he didn't always remember my daughter's name, seemed to remember the 1930s better than what happened the day before, didn't remember my dog's name but remembered the name of the dog at his father's factory. Is that typical?"

"Yes," Gorbien says. "Long-term memories, even in people with very advanced cognitive impairment, tend to stay intact for quite some time. Often, people with Alzheimer's and other dementias become nonverbal at the end, so we don't know what they might remember, because they can't speak."

"How much awareness does a patient have that he's losing his memory?" I ask. "My father, long before he met you, used to play at being 'senile,' at having forgotten things, and I always wondered if he had noticed some memory loss and was trying to make it into a joke."

"Some people come into the office the first time they lose a set of keys and say, 'Oh my God, I have Alzheimer's,'" says Gorbien. "Many people don't have that awareness at all. Your father was a highly intelligent man who was a quiet but astute observer. He was probably aware that he was having cognitive changes.

"Was he a happy man throughout his life, your father?" Gorbien asks me.

"When he was in control of his situation, he seemed to be," I say. "It's hard for me to say for sure, because he had me relatively late. He was forty-two, which doesn't seem old to me now, but by the time I was a functioning and aware kid, most of the things people talk about when they discuss my father, they're talking about someone I just saw glimpses of. And the person I've been learning about is someone I only sort of recognize."

"Did the family think of your father as being depressed?"

"Certainly toward the end, it was difficult to avoid thinking that. But the more I look into his life, the more I am beginning to wonder if he might not have been living his life pretty much the way he wanted to live it."

"Was he proud of his career?"

"Absolutely. He would always talk about how radiology was like detective work, about how many X-rays he could read and how fast, how he could finish faster than anyone at work. It made me want to be the fastest at everything I did."

"What about regrets?"

I think about the book my father never wrote. I begin to mention it, then stop, now wondering if it really was his regret, or whether it is more mine than it ever was my father's.

"Who can say?" I ask, then, "Is this an interesting job for you?"

"I love it. There's no such thing as an uninteresting family."

"But toward the twilight, it's not too bleak or grim?"

"No. Yesterday a patient with whom I had forged a very strong friendship died. It was a horrible day. Sometimes, I become friends with my patients, and I don't think that's a bad thing. Everyone in medicine looks at everyone else's specialty and says, 'Oh my God, I wouldn't do that.' I couldn't sit over a microscope and I couldn't sit in front of a view box, because I need to talk to people. So I love what I do. I love the stories."

"He never talked to you about writing a book, did he?" I finally ask.

"No," Gorbien says. "Some patients seem awfully hungry for conversation, and he certainly never seemed hungry for conversation. He never talked to me about much of anything."

2003

For three years, I've been living in New York with Beate. We've been married for about a year now, and I've been working full-time as a magazine editor, but I have also been getting up every morning to write fiction before I take the subway downtown. Ever since I've moved away from Chicago and recovered from a strange illness I had my first year in Manhattan, I've been able to write with greater focus and intensity. I've finished a draft of a novel set in my old Chicago neighborhood. It's about small lives playing out against the backdrop of a key but sometimes overlooked historical incident. Not the Bonus March and the transition from the Hoover twenties to the Roosevelt thirties, but the Iranian hostage crisis and the transition from the Carter seventies to the Reagan eighties. I have sent the manuscript to a couple of literary agents, but I haven't heard back from them yet.

I haven't been going back to Chicago to visit my folks as much as I probably should. I've never liked flying, even less so after 9/11, and the anxiety I feel on airplanes compounds the dread I feel about visiting Mozart Street, where nothing seems to change other than the slow, methodical decline that persists no matter how often I visit. However old I am, I always feel the same age when I'm in Chicago, and I haven't liked feeling that age for a long time.

I've been visiting Chicago for a couple of days and haven't slept much. Last night, my father kept calling out from his bedroom for my mother, and after I ran down the hall, he told me to wake my mom and go back to bed. When I refused ("Let her sleep, Dad; let her sleep for just a couple minutes"), he said he was losing sensation in one of his arms and feared he was having a stroke; when I said that

I would call his doctor or an ambulance, he said the feeling in his arm was returning.

In the morning, I'm in the kitchen with my parents and we are discussing what happened last night. "I had a TIA," my father says—a transient ischemic attack, a mini-stroke. "Well then, we have to call the doctor," I say, but my father says no. "If you had a mini-stroke, we have to call him," I repeat. "No," my father says, "maybe later." "No, not later," I say. "We have to call now." I get Dr. Gorbien on the phone, and he asks if I can stay on the other line while he talks to my dad.

"Do you think you had a TIA, Dr. Langer?" he asks.

"Hell yes, I know I did," my dad says.

Then my father needs to see him today, the doctor says. And as they debate, Gorbien's voice becomes more curt and impatient.

No, my father keeps saying, he doesn't have to go in.

"If you had a TIA, I need to see you."

"No, it's under control now; it's under control."

"Goodbye, Dr. Langer," Gorbien finally says, and after he has hung up, I go back downstairs. I tell my father that he needs to see the doctor. Today. "No," he says. "Dad," I say, "you have to; you can't put it off." "I'll do it tomorrow," he says. "No," I say, "not tomorrow. It can't wait until tomorrow. I'll go with you today." "You can go with me tomorrow," he says.

I feel my temper rising. I don't know how to get angry. I don't know how to raise my voice. I don't know how to yell. I've never been able to do it; whenever I have tried, it has always sounded fake to me. But now my cheeks flush and my heart beats fast, and I feel a lifetime of frustration beginning to rise from inside me—all the arguments we never had, all the words we never spoke.

"Today," I say.

"Shut up," my father tells me. "Would you just shut up?"

"Come on, don't tell me to shut up."

"Shut up," my father says again.

"Stop telling me to shut up. Can't you talk to me with a little more respect?"

Respect. The word slips out, a word I didn't really know I was thinking of. My voice sounds unfamiliar and also vaguely ridiculous to me, like I'm some character on *The Sopranos*—demanding respect from a sick man in a wheelchair. But apparently, it's something I've been seeking for a long time.

"Tomorrow," my father says again.

"No," I say, my voice getting louder, "not tomorrow. I will not be here tomorrow. I'm going home tomorrow. I don't live here anymore. We can't always say tomorrow; we can't always wait. We can't stay detached the whole time; sometimes we have to engage. Sometimes it's not tomorrow; sometimes it's today. Sometimes you have to move *today.*"

My father doesn't say anything.

I walk out the front door, heart still racing, cheeks still hot. I walk all the way to the water fountain at Chippewa Park on Sacramento Avenue, which has been where I've always walked to find solace. For some reason, the water tastes colder here than the water from any other fountain I've tried. I take a long drink, then a deep breath, wait for my heart to slow. I don't cry, though; I still haven't learned how to do that.

When I get back to the house, my father says he has made an appointment to see his doctor. "So," he asks, "does that make you happy?"

Several weeks later, I'm back in town and my father is being discharged from a nursing facility in north Evanston. It's an upscale nursing home; there's even a grand piano here, and my mother says the meals are decent, but the place still seems grim. In the commissary, a woman in a hospital gown continually calls out for a nurse, even when there's one right beside her.

My mother will be busy for the next hour or so dealing with paperwork, so she has asked me to drive back to Mozart Street ahead of her to make sure we're prepared for my father's return. I buy some medicine at the Osco drugstore. Then I go inside my parents' house to wait.

The house is so quiet, so peaceful, and I feel guilty that it's taken my father's trip to a nursing home for me to feel this sense of calm here. But the solitude lasts for only a few minutes before I see the Medi-Car pulling up and a paramedic opening the rear door to wheel out my dad. While I am watching the paramedic push my father's wheelchair toward the house, my mother following behind, I check my e-mail using my cell phone—there is a message from a literary agent in New York. The subject heading reads "I love your novel." I briefly read the e-mail, then go downstairs to open the front door for my father.

WEST BRANCH, IOWA

In winter, a trip from Chicago to West Branch, where the Herbert Hoover Presidential Library and Museum is located, takes place mostly amid a snow-white, predominantly featureless landscape with a pervasive bovine aroma. The distance is 232 miles, most of it on I-88 and I-80. The longest drive I ever took with my father was from Chicago to Madison, Wisconsin. We drove there with the rest of the family, bought ice-cream cones, looked briefly at the Edge-water, the hotel that he said his uncle Harry Bell had owned. Then we turned around and came home. The whole trip took about eight hours and I was carsick by the end of it—my father driving, as always, with one foot on each pedal.

My dad liked driving, liked being at the steering wheel of his Fords, but he rarely liked driving long distances. "There's no good way to get there," he'd say about anyplace he thought was too far. The thirty miles to my uncle Harry and aunt Faye's house on 114th Street was the limit. My dad often measured distances by whether they were of a reasonable length or too long, the latter of which he termed "farther than Faye's."

Today, I'm sitting in the passenger seat of a BMW and the GPS indicates the route we are taking. Long stretches of road pass without any towns being listed at all. This ride along interstates—frozen, barren cornfields, flat roads, big gray-blue sky—is the trip I would have taken with my father, or for my father. It is the trip we began talking about in the 1970s and were still discussing in 2005, the key research trip my father would take for his Bonus March book. My brother, Bradley, is with me today instead, and that's fitting. My brother is twelve years older than I, and he did much of what one traditionally expects fathers to do with sons—teaching me to ride a bicycle, taking me to baseball games at Comiskey Park, flinging the football around in the living room, playing catch outside, helping with algebra homework. No, he didn't go to parent-teacher conferences in grade school or high school or inspect my report cards, but then again, neither did my folks. One advantage of attending high school in Evanston and using my sister's address to gain free admission to the public school there was that my sister delivered my report cards to me, and I made sure the mediocre ones never quite made it to my parents.

In 1972, when my brother returned from his first semester at McGill University, in Montreal (my dad's idea, or so he said—a good way to dodge Vietnam), he came to my classroom to pick me up, and all the kids and teachers thought he was my dad. He took me on my first camping trip with his then girlfriend, Ellen, and a college buddy, out in Hoot Woods in southern Indiana, where we searched for salamanders and elusive blue fireflies. Outside Spencer, Indiana, we stopped at a Union 76 filling station, where the attendant pumped our gas, then looked at me sitting in the backseat. "That your boy?" he asked my brother.

When I was a teenager, my tastes became my brother's. I didn't read history books or *Commentary* or *Punch* like my dad. I cringed at the BBC comedy and news shows he listened to. I didn't listen to the bagpipe music or Peggy Lee songs my father enjoyed; I listened to Dylan, Lennon, the Band, the Stones. I worshiped Woody Allen, listened to comedy albums by George Carlin and the Congress of Wonders, read Calvin Trillin and Seymour Britchky, watched Bears and Sox games, *Monty Python, Fawlty Towers,* and *The Prisoner.* My brother's laconic speech patterns, equal parts Seymour Sidney Langer, George Carlin, and W. C. Fields, became mine, too: "Whatever"; "I'll be home when I'm home"; "It's probably garbage."

In 2000, while I was planning my move from Chicago to New York, my father said to me, "People never move to get away *to* someplace; they only move to get away *from* someplace," a statement that probably made sense coming from a man whose father had left the old country for America and who stayed in the same house for nearly fifty years, though to me, it seemed like a cynical way to view a desire to move on.

Shortly after I moved, my father was still working at the U of I, and in New York, I began suffering from an unrelenting illness—fevers, dizziness, a wicked sore throat, a tennis ball–size lump in my neck, drenching night sweats. Rooms I entered seemed darker than I remembered them. Walking along Morningside Drive, I would lose my balance, then stop to right myself before moving on. A doctor at Columbia said the symptoms would soon subside, but they didn't. Too much free time and easy access to WebMD turned apprehension into panic—some symptoms corresponded with tuberculosis, and I, the writer who has always liked symmetries and ironic coincidences, thought this symmetry would be appropriate: the son of a tuberculosis expert felled by TB. I spent sleepless, sweaty nights on the couch in a drab university-owned one-bedroom apartment on West 119th Street, sometimes leaving the door open partway at night when I felt particularly ill, hoping that, if I didn't wake up, somebody would push open the door and find me and revive me. I finally called my father, the doctor who never saw doctors and nearly always advised against seeing one.

"Call your brother," he said.

And when my condition still didn't improve and after my sister and mother both visited New York and viewed the growing lump in my neck, I went back to Chicago for tests. But my brother was the one who took me to the specialists, arranged the terrifying MRI ("It's nothing; they just put you in a tube for a while"), and introduced me to purportedly talented physicians, some of whom had remarkably poor bedside manners. "Do you know the clinical manifestations of mad cow disease?" one doctor asked another in reference to my condition while I was within earshot. Meanwhile, another jammed a needle into my unanesthetized neck for a biopsy. My brother arranged follow-up appointments as I lay on the couch at my parents' house waiting for my fevers and swelling to subside, wondering if they ever would, while my dad upbraided his thirty-three-year-old son for loafing around his house and not driving my mother to the Harold Washington Library to return overdue books. When I told him I had just undergone an MRI and was awaiting biopsy results, he asked me if I knew "how much those things cost." The affliction turned out to be some mutant form of strep; my brother dealt with the prescriptions.

My brother, also a radiologist, is currently medical director of Cook County Hospital, and my father, who spent Sunday dinners talking shop with him, often bragged of his elder son's position. "Do you know your brother runs the whole hospital over there?" he'd ask me. "Do you know he runs that whole joint?" My dad often overstated the accomplishments of others, his words serving both to flatter them and make them feel inadequate, for they would know they had not quite done everything my father credited them with doing—like when he said that Sammy Berkman invented Kayo or was chairman of the board of Dow; like when he wrote a speech that my sister delivered at my wedding, which he was unable to attend because of his health, saying that someday soon, he would expect to see me win the Nobel Prize for Literature and for Beate to run the United Nations; like, I'm thinking now, when he said his father was a mule skinner in World War I, or that he had a cousin who fought the Russians for the Polish army, or that his name was changed to fool the dybbuk; like, I'm thinking, when he said he would write a book about the Bonus March.

Just weeks after my father retired from medicine, he started talking about going back part-time, though he never did. As I sit in the car and my brother drives west on I-88, I ask why he thinks our father finally did retire, when he seemed to love his job so much. Was it his physical condition? Or his mental state? Had he perhaps started misreading X-rays?

Absolutely not, my brother says; the reasons were purely physical. It just became too much for him to get down the stairs and outside, to drive all the way south down Ashland Avenue, park the car, walk to his office—too much ground to cover, too much strain on his joints. Today, my brother works just blocks away from the hospital where my dad worked. He trained at the U of I, knows all my father's former colleagues; if there had been any sign of my father deteriorating mentally, the first call anyone would have made would have been to my brother.

But what about my father's X-ray-reading skills? I ask. Was he every bit as talented as he suggested? Or was there some self-mythologizing involved here? No, he was the best, my brother says. Although my brother tends toward understatement, when he speaks of my father's talents as a physician, his tone is that of a Chicago basketball fan discussing Michael Jordan: "He was legendary. For what he did, no one could touch him."

Like my dad, my brother likes to drive, but for longer distances. He and I used to take long rides like this in the car—up Sheridan Road on Sundays, turning around at Highland Park, sometimes stopping to peer in the windows of exotic auto dealerships or to get lunch at a deli, then heading back to our folks' house while I fiddled with his radio; we'd drive to the Horicon Marsh to see shorebirds, and to the Indiana Dunes and back. We haven't taken a drive like this in years—my daughter's two; his is approaching her eighth birthday. Nothing on the radio I want to listen to today, though; few songs on his iPod that I want to hear—one Talking Heads track ("Warning Sign") and I shut it off.

Across the Mississippi River, the view out the window begins to change subtly—fewer highway billboards and road signs, and those that are here are farther away from the road. This is the small-town Midwest, somewhere you can imagine American dreams being born—Jack and Jill supermarkets, main streets, green dinosaurs poised in front of Sinclair gas stations, the sort of landscape from which Herbert Hoover emerged, son of a Quaker blacksmith and a schoolteacher, who went on to become president of the United States, then, following the 1929 crash and the Bonus March, lost in a landslide to FDR.

As we approach West Branch, we tune in the local AM radio station, which talks up the Hoover Presidential Library and site— visitors effuse about how much more there is to do and see than they would have expected: Hoover's two-room birthplace cottage, the Friends Meetinghouse, the blacksmith shop where Hoover's father, Jesse, plied his trade.

The following morning, when we turn into the parking lot of the Hoover Presidential Library for our first day of research, the limestone walls suggest less the majesty of the presidency than the somber functionality of a funeral home. "Piser's," my father would no doubt have said, referencing the Piser Weinstein memorial chapel in

Chicago, a word he used to describe any drab item or setting. "What do you think of those drapes, Dad?" "Piser's." "What did you think of that restaurant?" "It looked like Piser's in there."

The research room is clean, quiet—low ceilings, fluorescents overhead, speckled gray carpet, nothing like Piser's really. The water in the fountain outside tastes of limestone or rust and its harsh aftertaste is a favorite topic of discussion among the librarians. Not many researchers here over the course of the day. Someone walks in to ask what part Hoover's family played in the Underground Railroad. Men and women in park rangers' uniforms wander in to chat. One librarian tells us this is one of their busier days. "It's not usually like this in winter," he says enthusiastically. "This is more like a day in summer." "How often do researchers come in here to request materials about the Bonus Army?" I ask him. "Maybe once or twice a year," he says.

My brother and I take our seats at one of the long wooden tables and plug in our laptops. A librarian rolls in a cart with seven file boxes containing newspaper clippings, correspondence, depositions, criminal reports. My brother and I split the files. My father was addicted to his work, but my brother says he sometimes sees radiology as more of a trade than an art, and even though he hasn't read about the Bonus Army since he wrote his high school research paper about it (Bradley's tastes tend toward novels by Patricia Highsmith and Andrew Vachss, and on our trip he has been reading Joe Orton's *Loot*), he dives into the work. He says he doesn't really expect to learn anything new about our dad here, but he's always up for a trip and a diversion. And if educating himself about the Bonus March provides it, so much the better.

"Here's MacArthur's testimony," he says, setting aside a copy of the remarks the general made before the press in the immediate aftermath of the expulsion of the Bonus Army ("I think this is the first riot I ever was in or ever saw in which there was no real bloodshed"). "Here's a song somebody wrote about the Bonus Army," Bradley says, passing me sheet music for a song entitled "Oh, Congress, It Is Up to You," by Morris Siegel. He thumbs through a series of newspaper clippings. "Newspaper articles are boring," he says. "They all say the same thing."

As we read, I again wonder what sort of book my father might have written. And then as I page through depositions, I begin to think about where exactly my father would have stayed in West Branch, Iowa, anyway. What lodgings would have been favored by the man who stayed at the Stanford Court or the Fairmont in San Francisco, in New York at the Plaza or the Regency, not too far from the Waldorf-Astoria, where both MacArthur and Hoover lived following their retirements? Would my father have checked into Iowa City's slick Hotel Vetro, where my brother and I are staying? As my dad would probably have put it, "Hell no." Would he have stayed at some Days Inn in downtown West Branch, such as it is, driving his Crown Vic back and forth to the library, investigating the exhibits? When did he see exhibits? Did he ever go to the Chicago Historical Society with me? Didn't he usually sit in the car and wait for me and my mom to emerge? The only museum visits I remember took place during the brief periods between parking the car in the Field Museum or Shedd Aquarium lot and walking to Soldier Field for Chicago Bears games—journeys so quick, we never bothered checking our coats, just walked in through the front door and out through the back. Fast, as always. *Is it done? Are you on your way in or on your way out?* Accelerator, brake, accelerator, brake.

At lunchtime, the library closes, and we take the opportunity to view an exhibit about Herbert Hoover's life and career. The Bonus Army receives scant attention; when this subject does come up (a wall with photographs and some text is devoted to it), Hoover is depicted as the victim of MacArthur's ego: "The president is blamed, even though MacArthur disobeyed White House commands." In the twenty-two-minute biographical video about Hoover that screens in an auditorium where my brother and I are the only spectators, the Bonus Army is represented by only a couple of unexplained images.

We return to our seats in the library. My mother has still been theorizing that my father could have written his book without going to Iowa ("He could have done it all on the Internet if he'd learned how to use it"), but the wealth of material here gives lie to the notion. Correspondence, telegrams, handwritten letters on notebook paper, editorial cartoons, a letter from Hoover himself with an actual H.H. signature—none of this has been digitized. No, he would have had to come here. Or I would have had to come with a suitcase full of quarters.

Which documents would interest him? I can't imagine him giving close attention to many, but I can see him, sort of, working here. He's paging through them one after the other, licking his thumb, the same as with X-rays: *This one I can use; this one I can't.* Until he finishes, and he can set the pile aside and clean his desk.

Which of the historical figures would my father have identified with? Certainly not with Hoover, who, even in the documents here, is either a willing participant in the forced expulsion of the veterans or MacArthur's pawn. And Hoover's childhood was so opposed to my father's—so American, so midwestern, so, well, goyish, my father would have said—picking potato bugs to earn money for Fourth of July fireworks, sitting in the lap of his mother, who wore a Quaker bonnet as she sat in her rocking chair. How could my father have related to Hoover, represented here in the museum by a statue wearing a coat, tie, fedora, and wading boots, fly-fishing reel in one hand? My father never fished. Hardly a Jewish activity, like hunting or horseback riding or becoming president of the United States.

MacArthur? My dad admired or at least was interested in military men—when I was a kid, he would open the middle buttons of his shirt, stick his hand inside, and say he was Napoleon posing for a portrait. But what did my father have in common with the Little Rock–born general other than impatience and a short haircut?

The artistically inclined D.C. police chief Pelham Glassford may have had most in common with my dad, but I never heard of Glassford until I started my research.

And what, I wonder, would my father have made of an unsigned 1932 letter here in these files, one apparently written by Hoover's wife, Lou Henry, to their son Allan? In it, Mrs. Hoover offers her opinions of the Democratic presidential candidates her husband might face in the fall general election. She writes of FDR:

> Everyone exclaims that he is not strong enough possibly to do the work. Personally I should hate to have him run, just because you do not like to fight a man who is handicapped. (And of course nearly everyone, Democrat and Republican, say his illness is his greatest asset. People admire him for his grit in so largely overcoming such an affliction. And heaps of people would vote for him just because he has put up such a game fight for his health, even tho' they don't know much about his ability to run the Administrative end of our government.)

At last, here's a message my father would have understood: You can be governor of the state of New York, a veteran politician, former secretary of the navy. Or you can be the chief radiologist in the city of Chicago, professor at the University of Illinois; you can be husband, father of three, and people will still judge you for how you do or don't walk, how courageous you are for not giving up.

My brother and I comb through more files in search of something from Chicago, a personal connection, some way to see how my father might have learned about the march from a relative or family friend. There is a report on a demonstration in Union Park, on Ogden Avenue and Randolph Street, in the spring of 1932. My father was too young to attend and his father was probably too busy operating his soda-pop business. In the presidential papers are three files' worth of criminal charges that were used to bolster the federal government's assertion that many bonus marchers were lowlifes and rabble-rousers. No Langers here.

I read reports from undercover investigators infiltrating meetings of the Bonus Army faction of the Workers Ex-Servicemen's League, attended by Communists John Pace and Emmanuel Levin. In a report about a meeting held on July 2, 1932, reference is made to a "white man by the name of Lang, apparently a Russian," who made threatening remarks to his congressman. True, the man's hometown is listed as Milwaukee. But some Bonus Army vets used pseudonyms, and Lang is close to Langer, Milwaukee is close to Chicago, and the man spoke with a Russian accent. It could conceivably have been my grandfather or some other relative, I tell my brother, though I add, "It's still kind of a stretch."

"More than a stretch," my brother says.

When we pack up our laptops and leave the Hoover Presidential Library for the day, I talk to my brother about this being the trip I would have taken with or for our father, but, I ask, could he actually imagine our dad working through these documents? Would he have ever made it out here to West Branch even if he had been perfectly healthy? But my brother observes that maybe whether our father would or wouldn't have gone to Iowa isn't important. Despite what our dad maintained, if you want to write a book about the Bonus Army, you can't just go to the Hoover Presidential Library anyway; you have to see FDR's papers, too, and Glassford's, and maybe even MacArthur's. My father always spoke of the Hoover Library as if it housed the treasure trove of Bonus Army history, but even if he had come here, even if he had read every document in the file boxes my brother and I have been searching, he would have been nowhere near done with his research. And my father liked to know when things would be done.

"So why do you think he wanted to write about the Bonus March?" I ask my brother.

"The Bonus March is Rosebud," he says, using the name of

Charles Foster Kane's sled in *Citizen Kane*. It's a way into discussing our father's life, but in the end, its meaning will prove elusive. Writing the book was just a dream for my dad, not much different from my brother having once wanted to quarterback the Chicago Bears. We all have our own Bonus Marches; we all have interests or obsessions through which we view the world to make it more understandable to us. For my dad, the Bonus March was one; TB was another.

Ultimately, my brother says, the Bonus March book is probably more important to me than it was to our father; it was just something that would have made his life seem more fulfilling. It would have been something for him to do. It could have been anything, just something for him to look forward to, something so he wouldn't have had to sit in "that chair" all day long. It could have been a book about the Bonus March, or it could have been anything else.

I fear that my brother will prove to be right, but I still think there might be something more to it; I have nothing to back this up, though, except a hope, a gut feeling, and a sense of how stories are supposed to work, that they're supposed to lead to resolutions and definitive answers. But I have to follow my father's story where it does or doesn't go, not where I'd like to see it end up.

Spring is approaching, but here on the site of the Hoover Library, there is little sign of it. The lawns are frozen and dogs are frolicking on them. At the presidential grave site, marble tombstones are almost completely covered by snow; the only visible letters are the HE of Herbert and the LO of his wife, Lou Henry. *Hello*, they seem to be saying.

"Weird thing, death," my brother says.

SUMMER 2005

Conversations with my father have been getting even shorter since I've arrived at my parents' house with Beate to introduce them to their three-month-old granddaughter, Nora. When I was living in my last Chicago apartment, on Farragut Street, my father would call me, ask how I was doing, then add, "Is there anything I can do for you?" I could never come up with an answer, always thought the answer was supposed to be no anyway, so the conversation would pretty much end there and he'd say, "Do you want to talk to your mother?" These days, I'm lucky if I get even that far.

On the occasions when I called to tell him that Beate was pregnant, then that Nora had been born, he seemed pleased, but he only said something like "I think that's swell" before passing the phone to my mom. He's been in and out of the hospital and elder-care facilities lately, but the last time I called him at a hospital to see how he was doing, he just asked where my sister was and if I would tell her to call him.

"Does that mean you don't want to talk to me right now?" I asked.

"Hell yes," he said, and so I called my sister.

My dad can rarely make it upstairs anymore to his old bedroom. There's a hospital bed in the den, where my playpen once was, pills and a first-aid kit on the end table where my record player used to be. Sometimes he'll stay all night in his wheelchair, sleep in the kitchen, head on the table. My mother had a motorized chair installed to get him upstairs and down, but when he was mobile enough to get in and out of it easily, he refused to use it, just stared at it darkly, as if regarding some bleak future. His face rarely changes expressions, and he seems more distant than ever, as if gazing at a world that he's no longer a part of. Sometimes, my mother will wheel him out onto the back porch, where there's now an elevator; she'll take him to the yard and work in the garden while he sits at the picnic table. He wears a flannel shirt when it's cool outside, shorts when the weather's warmer, a baseball cap to protect him from the sun—all items of clothing my father never wore before he retired, not even on weekends. The skin on his arms is browned, a side effect of one of the medications he is taking.

Five days a week, my father's home-care worker, Elena, comes to help my mom. Elena is just about the only home-care worker my mother has been able to tolerate having in her house. Most of the other workers I met earlier seemed lethargic and bored—marking time for the paycheck at the end of the week. They sat with my dad, read books, watched TV. In the logbook, where I could read how my father passed his days—reading, gazing out the window, sketching, speaking little, if at all—one worker wrote snarkily that she spent one day sitting with my father, listening to the radio: "It was soooooooooo interesting."

Today, when my mother opens the door and sees her granddaughter, she quickly takes Nora in her arms and holds her tightly, almost as if she's afraid she will drop her. She takes Nora to my dad, who smiles for a moment, but soon the smile passes—it seems as if he's smiling only because it's expected, to reassure us that his condition, if poor, is nonetheless stable. My mother places Nora in his lap. "See," she says, using the nickname "See" for Seymour. "See, this is Nora." But my dad isn't steady enough to hold Nora, so my mom holds their granddaughter for him in his lap.

I spend a good part of these few days in Chicago with Beate and Nora sitting on the front stoop of the house, the same front stoop where my father once greeted or avoided the neighbors, sat in a lawn chair reading *Commentary* or *Punch*, drinking scotch from a glass tumbler, shining his shoes with Kiwi polish and rags that he kept in a barium barrel, waiting for my mother to call him in for dinner.

The last time I was here—in the spring, shortly before Nora was born—I bought my dad a tape recorder so that, even if he couldn't hold a pen for a long time, maybe he could start work on a book—if not the weighty, researched tome we had discussed for so many years, at least maybe a memoir. But he had trouble operating the record and rewind functions of the machine. He kept fumbling with it, speaking into it, recording, erasing, recording, erasing, and all he kept saying into the microphone was that line from the old Ink Spots song "We Three": "We three, we're all alone . . ." My mother has suggested that he might be able to write by using a computer, but when I've shown him how to type on my laptop, he writes the same sentence: "We three, we're all alone . . ."

On the last day of our trip to Chicago, I take photographs and little movies of Nora with my mother and father. I wonder if this will be the only time she will see her grandfather. Apparently, this thought is on my father's mind, too. As I'm taking photographs, he wheels toward me and says, "Make sure I'm in some of those pictures."

"I will," I say. "You already are."

OASIS LANGER

It's a particularly warm autumn afternoon in New York, just moments before I will pick Nora up from preschool, and I am sitting on the front stoop of our apartment building on Duke Ellington Boulevard when I feel my phone vibrating in my pocket.

"Hello?"

"Oasis Langer!"

"What?"

"Oasis Langer!"

It's my uncle Jerome. He has been rummaging through his boxes and files and says he has finally found my grandfather's "Declaration of Intention" document, which he filed shortly after his arrival in America. The name listed on the document is not Samuel, but Oasis, Jerome says—he'll give me a copy of it when I'm in town.

The next time I'm in Chicago, I sit at the kitchen table, which my mother has set with bagels, cream cheese, orange juice, a plate of fruit, and coffee for my uncle. But when Jerome arrives and sits at the table, he doesn't take anything. He's here for business; he's got someplace to go right after he's done talking to me; he's in a rush.

He places before me on the table the items he's found—my father's 1938 diploma from Sumner Elementary School, and a copy of the 1915 declaration form from the U.S. Department of Labor for my grandfather, whose name is listed not as Oasis but *Osias,* and whose foreign residence is listed as Rachin, Austria, a small rural village in the former region of Galicia in what is now Ukraine. Rachin is located south of Lvov, not Langerdorf, a town my dad seems to have made up.

> I, Osias Langer, aged 21 years, occupation Laborer, do declare on my oath that my personal description is: Color white, complexion ruddy, height 5 feet 4 inches, weight 130 pounds, color of hair black, color of eyes brown. . . . I now reside at 714 Laflin Street, Chicago, Illinois. I emigrated to the United States from Antwerp, Belgium on the vessel Finland.

"Isn't that somethin'?" Jerome Langer asks me, then answers his own question. "How about that? That's somethin'. That's a clue."

After Jerome leaves, I write another letter to the National Personnel Records Center in St. Louis, asking if there might be a record not for a Samuel Langer, but for an Osias Langer of Chicago, who worked as a mule skinner during World War I.

AUTUMN 2005

My father had a stroke on Friday and hasn't regained consciousness. My mother has reported that he has clutched her hand a couple of times and that he has opened his eyes on one or two occasions, but it doesn't seem as if he will wake up. My mother is debating whether to place him in a hospice or a nursing home, or to have him stay at the house. She has asked his doctors how long he has. They haven't told her anything specific, but I've told Beate that I should probably go to Chicago for a few days anyway. "I keep hoping for a miracle," my mother says. Still, I reluctantly pack my dress shoes, a black suit, and my black overcoat—just in case—and fly from La Guardia to O'Hare.

In Chicago, the handicapped space is still out in front of my parents' house, even though my mother has already given my dad's car to my uncle Jerome. I park my rental car across the street and make sure to unpack my black suit and shoes and leave them in the trunk before I take out my suitcase, not wanting to bring bad luck into the house. If I wind up wearing the suit, I hope my mother won't wonder why I thought to bring it along.

Inside the house, my mother and I chat for a while, but whatever we discuss fades from memory almost immediately. I feel exhausted, bitter-cold, like a fever is coming on. My mom and I watch the news, but I'm too tired to pay attention. We make plans to visit my father in the hospital in the morning. I go upstairs to my old bedroom and fall asleep in my clothes.

I have been sleeping soundly for just a little over an hour when I hear the telephone ring. Already I know what the ring means. I have been expecting this telephone call for days. A week ago, when my friend Paul called to chat in the middle of the night, I already assumed the ringing phone meant my father was gone.

I hear my mother pick up her phone and talk quietly. I hear her hang up. I hear silence. I hear her walk toward my room. I see her standing in the doorway. I don't even process the words she uses—whatever she says, the moment after she says it, every part of me feels even colder than before.

The hospital is desolate at one in the morning. The usual entrance from the garage is closed. When we get inside, we meet a nurse named Christina; she's young, pretty in a Bible camp sort of way. She tells us my father looked very peaceful, asks if we want to see him one last time.

Someone's lying beneath the sheets in room 748, but it doesn't look like my father. Of course his body is there, but he seems to be wearing a mask—mouth open, eyes closed. His soul, his spirit, whatever animated him, has already fled. The last thing my father told my mother when she saw him on Friday was for her to leave the hospital when she had the chance, get out before she got caught in traffic. That was my father's last piece of advice, so typically practical. Not "Rosebud" or "Bonus March." Just "Get out so you can beat traffic." *How long will you be here? Are you on your way in or on your way out?*

My mother doesn't want to stay in this room. Me, neither. She and I carry out my dad's belongings—his glasses, his shirts, his radio, his cap—in two big clear plastic bags. In the family room, a nurse opens the doors to an entertainment center.

Do we want to watch TV, the nurse asks.

No.

My mother tries to call my father's brother, but she keeps misdialing. I call Jerome, and, though his voice is crackly—it's late and he has the flu and has been popping cough medicine and lozenges—he snaps into action. Always the *macher*. Always the man who can get things done. I give my mother the phone and Jerome starts asking questions: What sort of service do we want? Do we want it at the graveside? A service in a chapel? Piser Weinstein? Shalom?

"I don't know, Jerry," my mom keeps saying. "I just don't know."

Jerome says he'll pick us up at nine in the morning and take us to Shalom. No, he says, not Waldheim, definitely not Waldheim, definitely not that place where my grandparents are buried.

"No one wants to go to Waldheim anymore," Jerome Langer says. "It's too depressing."

The chaplain, who is younger than I and looks like he might have been a stoner in high school, enters the room and starts asking questions about my father, tells us he's sorry for our loss, usual stuff, words you hear on TV shows. No, we say, he wasn't a religious man. No, we don't want the chaplain to say a blessing. Before we leave, my mother goes into the room to take one last look at my dad. I go in with her, but this time I don't look. I keep my eyes focused on a point in space.

We walk out of the hospital and get into my car. Maybe it's two in the morning. We try paying for parking, but the machine won't accept my credit card. A voice over the intercom says we should come to the gate, but no one's there to take our money, and so we just drive out into the night. I'm reminded of a line from my favorite Martin Scorsese movie, *After Hours:* "Different rules apply when it gets this late."

As we turn onto Harrison Street, I hear my cell phone ringing. My brother's calling; he says he's on his way. He meets us in front of the Rush parking lot, gets in my car, and we drive around the city, going nowhere in particular, just driving around this block and that, taking a long circuitous route, eventually winding up at my brother's building.

Bradley says he will come over to the house tomorrow morning; then we will go to Shalom to make arrangements. We leave him at his apartment and then my mother and I drive home. I talk about how depressed my father had seemed these last years, about how he wouldn't have been happy in a hospice, about how good it was that he had spent most of his time at home, about how my mother may finally be able to get some rest.

"But I didn't want that," my mother says. "I didn't want *that*."

The next morning, my brother, mother, uncle, and I drive to Shalom Memorial Park. It's oddly beautiful here, perfect autumn, fruits of osage orange trees everywhere. We'll be meeting the head of the funeral home. He's a good guy, Jerome says, but still, we should watch out for him; still, he's a salesman; still, at the end of the day, he knows how to make a buck, and if you don't believe that, the guy has his own private jet.

"Whatever," Bradley says, but Jerome says no: "You can't say 'whatever' to these guys, Bradley. If they hear you saying 'whatever,' they charge you more."

Whatever.

We are ushered into a tiny conference room. There seems to be barely enough oxygen for all of us to breathe, and I spend half of the time getting up and going to the bathroom, getting up to get a drink from the fountain, getting up to get some air, getting up to make phone calls.

In the room, the particulars of my father's funeral are debated. Do we want pallbearers? No, no pallbearers, says my brother. "You gotta have pallbearers," Jerome says. Okay, six pallbearers. Do we want an Orthodox rabbi or a Conservative or a Reform rabbi? A male or a female rabbi? We don't care what rabbi, just not Orthodox, my brother says. "A male rabbi," says my uncle. "It's gotta be male." Do we want just one plot or two for the price of one, since prices will go up in January? Sure, two, why not. This is smart, we are told, because now we'll get two plots for three years at no interest.

One of the least Jewish-looking Jewish men I've ever seen arrives, a doughy guy who happens to be the funeral director. He has a checklist, but my brother is taking charge. Channeling my dad, he says our one object is "to get the hell out of here as soon as possible." But the funeral director still needs to tick off items. Do we need a limo? No. Service at the chapel? No. Gloves for the pallbearers? No. How many copies of the Death Notice do we need? What do we want the death notice to say? He takes a pen and a pad of paper and begins suggesting adjectives. Is "loving father" okay? Not everybody wants to use the word *loving,* he says. "Loving father" is okay? Good. How about "cherished friend"? Okay. How about "devoted husband"? Fine. How about "respected colleague," too, my mother suggests. The funeral director says he's never heard of anyone including the words *respected colleague* before, and he doesn't know how to spell *colleague.* My mother spells it for him.

I am heartened by the fact that, if my father is somewhere watching, this is the exact sort of scene that he, a man who always joked about funerals, a man who described drapes by saying they looked like they belonged at Piser's funeral home, a man who always turned first to the obituary page, would find uproarious.

The funeral director asks if we know what the headstone will say when it will be unveiled; we don't need to decide right away.

"Loved by all who knew him," my mother offers as a first suggestion. And though I like the sound of the phrase, I don't know if it means I knew my father completely or not at all.

When we get home, the phone is already ringing. Jerome is on the line; he's ordering cold cuts. How many people will be attending shiva? How much food will we need? How many trays?

The day of the funeral turns out to be lovely, too—the sun peeks out between the branches of the osage orange trees. There are six pallbearers, but I'm not one of them; I can't bring myself to do it. The rabbi wears a Scooby-Doo tie; when I ask why he's wearing it, he says it's important to add levity to grave situations. It seems as though just about all the people who were close to my father are here—my brother, my sister, my mom; the doctors and technicians my father worked with at the U of I; his brother, Jerome; his friends from Marshall High, Lenny and Sue Primer, Seymour and Marlene Levine; his cousins Pepi Bernstein, Frances Corwin, Jerry and Pepi Singer. "Your father was a good man," Jerry says. "He did right by us."

At the service, my sister speaks of two of the things my father loved most in life—getting a good parking space and reading. I talk about the things I remember my father liking, too—*Punch* magazine, English toffee, Myron & Phil's. And I talk, too, about the fact that at the end of his life, if he realized that he had worked for more than fifty years and that he would be surrounded by friends, colleagues, and family here, he might have looked down upon this scene and in his pleased but nonplussed fashion said, "Well, this didn't turn out half-bad." The rabbi says that this way of looking at my father's life is a good one; we should all be so lucky as to have a life that doesn't turn out half-bad. He says the Kaddish. Afterward, our West Rogers Park neighbors Rabbi Michael Small and his son, Rabbi Ari Small, shovel the dirt.

I don't head straight home after the funeral for shiva. Instead, I take the long way back, my best friend, Paul, in the passenger seat. We pass all the sites we used to frequent when we were in high school, all our hangouts. We even stop for a burger and shake at Homer's ice cream parlor. We used to drive by here at least once a week. Now I can't recall when the two of us were last in a car together.

The atmosphere back at the house is wrong somehow. It looks like one of my parents' old New Year's Eve or Halloween parties, as if everyone is still here but my father has lumbered up to bed to read Barbara Tuchman or watch *Benny Hill.* People are drinking soda pop, eating cold cuts. My cousin Paul is introducing himself to my friend Paul. "Good name," he says. Neighbors are stopping by— a woman my age whom I haven't seen since we were both children; Mr. Seruya from across the street. "Good days," he says, offering a Jewish blessing. "From now on, only good days."

In my parents' living room, my mother talks with the two rabbis—Rabbi Small and Rabbi Small. My mother discusses how this neighborhood is changing, how the Conservative Jews have moved out and all her neighbors are Orthodox now; so many Russian Jews live here now, too. But the elder Rabbi Small says no. A lot of the Russians have already moved out, too, he says. They've made their money and they've moved to the suburbs. Look around, he says; it's always changing. The rabbis are the last to leave, and after they go home, my mother and I are alone. She shakes her head, lets out a breath.

"What?" I ask.

"Your father had lots of plans," she says.

I don't remember her saying anything else; she leaves that thought unfinished. The next time I return to Chicago, she will show me the letter Barbara Tuchman sent to my father, and, in my own way, I will begin to try to finish that thought for her, to pay off that debt.

HYDE PARK, NEW YORK

The Franklin D. Roosevelt Presidential Library and Museum in Hyde Park, New York, looks like a Piser's memorial chapel from the outside, too. But the Arthur M. Schlesinger, Jr., Research Room resembles every other research library where I've been working, just a bit brighter—more fluorescents overhead. This should be my last trip to research the story of the Bonus Army. In the summer of 1935, over two hundred Bonus Army veterans lost their lives in the hurricane that hit Key West. In January 1936, the bonus bill passed, and in June, four years after the marchers first began arriving in D.C., checks started going out, nearly three million of them. The first was delivered to a veteran in a ceremony at Walter Reed Hospital.

The Roosevelt Museum's permanent exhibit doesn't contain much information about the Bonus Army. A brief film that plays in a small hall designed to resemble a typical 1930s home tells the official story—FDR's fireside chats inspire the nation; "We are saved," someone writes in a letter to the president; "Happy Days Are Here Again" plays on an antique radio. In a tiny imitation newsreel theater, images of the Depression are shown, but the one with smoke rising toward the Capitol receives no explanation. The only mention of the Bonus Army is offered in a wall display about the First Lady, where there is a clipping from a May 17, 1933, edition of *The New York Times* about Eleanor Roosevelt touring the Bonus camps: "Hoover sent his soldiers; Roosevelt sent his wife."

The librarian on duty asks what I'll be researching. "Oh, the Bonus Army," he says after I tell him; then he laughs. "You won't find much here."

The librarian asks if I've been to the Hoover Library. When I tell him I have, he says he might have some information on bonus legislation in transcripts of Democratic National Committee hearings, but not much else. Well, he says, I might as well have a look, since I came all this way.

The file boxes that the librarian finds are full of correspondence, pro- and anti-bonus legislation. There are telegrams, letters from some of the same people who also wrote to Hoover, and responses to the comments FDR made regarding the bonus bill in speeches and radio addresses. Once again, I am most affected by the stories of strangers, of people whose names have been forgotten, as faceless as images on X-rays: a mother from New Haven, Connecticut, who writes of picking through trash to support her family; a first grader whose parents work in a sock mill and who pleads for his father's bonus so that his family can move to the country; a little girl who asks FDR to sign the bonus bill, and to send her an autograph so she can frame it.

In the documentary I might have liked to film, this would be the right time for the eureka moment, the time when I actually find some letter that my father wrote as a child. No such luck. Nevertheless, I request a file for all letters written about the bonus by people with surnames beginning with *L*. No Langer here, either. Nothing from my father or his family. When he was a kid, he would have liked the stamps on these envelopes, though. By the time he was an adult, he would have lost interest in them and would have given them to me. Why? "For the hell of it," he'd say. Outside the library, it looks like a gorgeous day; I seem to have reached the end of my journey.

OSIAS

Evening is falling in New York and I've spent most of the day with Nora and Beate. We walked through Central Park, played in Riverside Park, ate lunch at Nora's favorite Chinese restaurant, bought cookies from the Hungarian Pastry Shop, snarfed them down across the street in the park of the Cathedral of St. John the Divine, watched peacocks stroll and squawk there. Nora always hates for days to end, but it's finally time to go home.

Once we're inside our apartment building, I stop in the hallway to open our mailbox. There's another letter from the National Personnel Records Center inside.

"I am enclosing a listing from our registry of all records with the first name Osias. As you can see, there is no match with the last name of Langer," an analyst writes. But then he allows for one other possibility: "It may be that he worked (as a mule skinner) with the military as a contract worker to haul materiel, but there does not appear to be a military personnel file for him."

No, I think, I probably will never be able to verify whether my grandfather ever served in World War I in any capacity or whether that fact influenced my father's interest in the Bonus March. But at the same time, the suggestion that my grandfather might have worked as a mule skinner but not as an official member of the army has the ring of truth. My cousin Sammy Berkman didn't invent Kayo as my dad had claimed, but he did work for the man who did; my cousin Harry didn't own the New Lawrence Hotel as my father said, but he did put together the deal for the man who did; my dad's name may or may not have been changed to Seymour to fool the dybbuk, but his birth certificate says "Sidney Langer" on it, and it was changed in his childhood. My uncle doesn't remember Sam Langer working as a bartender in a Capone-era speakeasy, but he does remember that his dad had been a bartender. Perhaps Sam Langer didn't serve in the U.S. Army as a mule skinner, but he performed that job as a civilian contractor. *Could be,* I hear my uncle Jerome's voice saying as I close the mailbox. And yet I keep wondering why the stories my father told me have turned out to be only partially true.

My father told me American Dream stories, rags-to-riches tales, stories like Horatio Alger's and Sammy Glick's. But he had to invent details in order to make them fit that narrative; apparently, he didn't think his own real stories were good enough. Clearly, I think as I walk upstairs, holding my daughter's hand, he didn't really believe in the myth. No, he believed in the story of the Bonus March—his version of it anyway, the one in which MacArthur's men crush the Bonus Army veterans and they never get paid. And my story of my father's life is a little like that, too. Sure, it's the story of a man who rose from the depths of the Depression to become a doctor, husband, father, and grandfather, but in my version, the one I've been telling anyway, he didn't achieve his dreams, either. He never wrote his Bonus March book.

Epilogue

Stories We Choose to Tell

I'll take the written word over your memory.

DR. SEYMOUR SIDNEY LANGER, family recording, 1964

MOZART STREET
(2008)

I

I'm forty years old now. My father has been gone for nearly three years. It's springtime and my daughter and I are in Chicago for a week's vacation while Beate is teaching in Indiana. I never saw my parents' childhood homes, only recall meeting one of my grandparents, and he died when I was six. I want Nora to know where and how I grew up, don't want her to feel the same sort of detachment I have often felt regarding my history.

During our trip, we've been reading some of my favorite books, the ones that my mom used to read to me when I was a kid: *The Plant Sitter, The Blueberry Pie Elf;* my mom has been singing to Nora the lullabies she sang to me ("Lazy Bones," "Go to Sleep Now, My Pumpkin," "Big Rock Candy Mountain"); we've gone to the Conrad Sulzer Library, where my mom has been volunteering, reading stories on Saturday mornings. She's still keeping her schedule full—the gym, English classes, lunches with her sister Faye. While we've been here, she has been staying up late to read *Adam Bede,* by George Eliot, and *Letters to a Student Revolutionary,* by Elizabeth Wong. The other day, I boasted to my mother that I had walked five miles. "Oh," she said, "almost as much as me."

Sometimes, the neighbors come by to see how she's doing. During the winter, her next-door neighbor Ari shovels her walk. His wife, Nachama, has invited her over for Shabbos dinner.

On this trip, Nora has been looking at photographs with my mother. "That's Oma," she says, using the German word for grandmother when she sees a picture of my mom. "That's Papa," she says when she sees a picture of me. "Who's that?" she asks when she sees a picture of my father. But even when we tell her, the information doesn't quite register. How do you tell a two-and-a-half-year-old that somebody she doesn't remember isn't here anymore?

I've been trying to talk to my mother about my dad, but she still doesn't seem to want to discuss him too much. She's the one persevering now, and it seems as if the only way she can keep moving forward is by not looking back. But I keep thinking that there must be something I've missed, that I've failed somehow. In my mother's stories, my father could always do anything he set his mind to doing: *Your father could read faster than anyone else. Your father read X-rays faster than anyone else. Your father, he was somethin' else.*

"You know," I finally tell my mother, "I've been thinking that dad might not have written his book even if he'd had all the time in the world to do it. Maybe it was just something to talk about, nothing he ever would have really done. Maybe it was more important for us than it was for him."

"Well," my mother says, "by the end, he couldn't do it anyway."

"Right," I say. "But even if he had been healthy. We always say that he would have done it if he had been healthy. But think about all the things that go into writing a book—could you imagine him actually going to Los Angeles or Washington or Iowa? We talked about him going there for years, and he never did it."

"Well, he could have gotten everything he needed through the Internet," my mother says. "That was my idea."

"Sure, but you can't write a whole history book just using the Internet. A writer has to interact with people. It's not like sitting in a room with X-rays. He would have had to engage, talk to people, interview them maybe."

"Well, your father wasn't an interviewer," my mother says.

"And he probably would have had to go to at least some of these places, at least travel to Washington, D.C. The last time he went to Washington was before I was born."

"No, your father wasn't a traveler," my mother says.

"And," I say, "he was always so impatient. He never liked staying anywhere for longer than he had to. Can you even imagine him spending days in libraries with books and microfilm?"

"Your father wasn't a researcher," my mother says.

"So," I say, "maybe he wouldn't have written the book even if he'd had all the time he needed."

"He was a good writer, though," she says. "The writing—that he could have done.

"Well," she finally says, "what difference does it make now anyway?"

II

Nora is asleep upstairs and I'm in the basement with my mother, who has agreed to help me look through some of her and my father's old belongings to see if we can find any clues to my dad's history. She seems to be slowly warming to the idea of talking about my father, but I still have the feeling that she'd prefer to keep everything boxed away. We rummage through old barium barrels that contain mementos of her early days with my dad—my dad liked to store things in barium barrels. Here's a smudged penny from 1933; here are results of my mother's civil service exam, playbills, matchbooks, wedding guest lists, invitations, envelopes, thank-you notes, a picture of my mom's father, Abe Herstein, accompanying a man-on-the-street interview with him in a 1952 newspaper, notes my mom wrote in the hospital shortly after my brother and sister were born, a 1959 rental-car receipt, a pair of argyle socks she knitted.

"Those are the socks I made for Dad," she says. "I did it surreptitiously at the office before we were married. But they never fit. I guess we can throw them away now. I hate to throw things out. Isn't that crazy? I hate to throw anything out."

We find more wedding invitations, envelopes, blank pieces of paper, road maps from my parents' East Coast honeymoon, a dried wedding corsage, artifacts from a trip to Yosemite—my mom now says she doesn't remember if my dad was even on that trip. We take the items we find and place them in piles on top of the billiard table.

"This kind of gives me the creeps," my mother says.

"So who was the saver?" I ask. "Did you save all this stuff?"

"I probably saved all of it," she says.

"But don't you think if you saved it, you would have done a better job?"

"I guess so," my mom says.

"Would you put stuff in a shoe box and stick it in a barium barrel? Does that sound like you?"

"No," my mother says. "I guess I wanted to save it, so your dad threw it all in here. It was probably your father's idea to put all this in his barium barrels; that was his shtick."

We find an old Kleenex, a matchbook from the restaurant Don the Beachcomber, another from a restaurant on Fisherman's Wharf in San Francisco.

"Is it safe to be keeping all these matchbooks?" I ask.

"I don't know. I've had them so long, I guess it's okay."

We find a bar of hotel soap, a pair of suspenders, a Kewpie doll.

"So," I ask, "you don't think we'll find anything down here that will tell us why he was interested in the Bonus March, do you?"

"I don't think so," my mother says.

"Think we'll ever find anything about it at all?"

"No."

"Anything about anybody serving in the military?"

"No."

"Polish generals? World War One?"

But my mom is already through with the topic. "We looked at this already," she says as she glances at another wedding invitation list. "Should I get a new shoe box to put some of this stuff in?"

"Up to you," I say.

III

The next morning, I'm getting dressed to prepare for our day. For our trip, I packed Nora's shirts and her pants and her socks and her underwear, also about a dozen of her books and her stroller and her stuffed blue bear and her orange plastic horse and her markers and her paper and her stamps. What I forgot to pack, however, were shirts and socks for myself.

Nora and I go into my parents' old bedroom. To me, the room is filled with memories of my father; to Nora, it's a playground. She takes the pillows and the sheets off the bed and heaps them on the floor; then she takes off her socks and she jumps up and down on the bed. "Nora! Nora! Jumping up and down!" she cries.

In this bedroom, the closets and drawers are still filled with my father's shirts and his socks and his whimsical ties. I take out one of his shirts, a light blue pinpoint oxford and a pair of his socks and place them on the bed. I don't wear the exact size shirt that my dad did—he was both a bit broader and a tiny bit shorter than I—but the shirts always fit well enough, and he liked loaning them to me. Before I'm able to change into the shirt, though, my mother walks into the room. She looks at the shirt I'm about to put on. I hear her let out a short breath.

217

"What?" I ask.

"The shirt," she says. "You wear the same size shirt as your father."

And I don't want to say that I just grabbed the shirt out of my dad's old closet because I forgot to pack enough clothes. I just say, "Yes, I do."

IV

Nora is in the basement laundry room, playing with my mother. She's riding my old red tricycle back and forth, past the wall where the black-and-white eight-by-ten photo of my father on his tricycle is still mounted. I'm on the second floor, looking for an article my father wrote that appeared in a medical journal when I was in high school. The file cabinets up here are filled with papers and memorabilia—in the *A* (for Adam) folder are grade school photographs of me, a copy of the honorable mention certificate I won for a grammar school art contest that my father helped me with.

In the *S* (for Seymour) folder, I find two copies of the article—an op-ed piece my father wrote about the need for chest X-rays to remain part of a standard physical workup. There's a picture of my dad in a white lab coat reading an X-ray, sneering and squinting like some combination of Lionel Barrymore and Robert De Niro. But the writing is functional, devoid of introspection, and there's nothing here I don't know. I thumb through the rest of the papers in the *S* folder. I find a letter from the U of I radiology department thanking him for his service. Tucked behind the letter are about half a dozen pages of lined white loose-leaf paper written in my father's instantly recognizable left-handed doctor's scrawl. The handwriting is shaky, though, the way it looked in his last few years, when holding a pen became difficult for him. My father had apparently begun writing something after he retired. But no, he didn't write about the Bonus March. These seem to be reminiscences of his days in medical school. On the top of one of the pages, there is even a working title—"The Humanity of Man." I begin to read my father's recollections of training with Eric Oldberg, a well-known Chicago physician who was head of neurosurgery when my dad was a med student.

Dr. Oldberg's morning rounds at the Illinois Neuropsychiatric Institute were very well attended. The flowing entourage of students was well aware that they were in the presence of greatness. On one particular morning in the Summer of 1949 the group entered a room on 3S. The resident presented the case—a young farm woman dying of inoperable glioblastoma multiforme. There was no hint of what she might have looked like before she was ill, but at that time she was shriveled, gaunt and looked more like a starved concentration camp victim than anything else. During the presentation she lay there, whimpering with tears running down her cheeks. Rather than question the resident or proceed to the next patient, Dr. O came over to her, held her, and in his quiet manner asked her if there was anything he could do for her. She continued crying and said, "All I want is some salt." Dr. O looked perplexed and didn't seem to understand. He looked over to Mrs. Ness, the head nurse who clued him in. It seemed that one of the residents had noted that this terminal woman had high blood pressure and had put her on a salt-free diet. Dr. O, aghast, dismayed, but still in control, quietly told Mrs. Ness to take her off the salt-free diet, went over to a tray and got a salt shaker and poured some salt into the hand of this woman who stopped crying and breathed more easily. With no further ado, we proceeded to the next patient.

I turn the page:

There was a rather poignant episode during rounds in the 50s. One of the residents was a very statuesque woman. All the people in rounds tried to get as close to Dr. O as possible during rounds and crowded around him. This particular morning, Dr. L crowded close to Dr. O. He kept looking away from her in his reserved manner and ended up against a wall. It was not until then that he and subsequently all concerned noted that there was a reason for her getting close to him. He noticed and quietly mentioned to her after rounds that she had nystagmus. She subsequently died of MS.

I turn another page:

The residents' quarters at INI bordered on the luxurious. There was a party held there against the rules. The party attracted a hungry, thirsty, lecherous crowd. The participants left beer cans, debris, and shoes and bras and rooms in disarray. Furniture was stacked to make room for a dance floor. None of this was cleaned up. The next morning, one of the nursing supervisors insisted on showing the "mess" to Dr. O. His only comment was "Have someone clean up the rooms." No one heard another word about the mess.

Six pages in, my father stopped writing.

As my mother and daughter play downstairs, I wander through the hallways of my parents' home, thinking about these words my father wrote, the snippet of a memoir he began. I wander through the hallway, where his white lab coat no longer hangs in a closet, through the kitchen, where my father no longer sits in the armchair at the head of the table, through the dining room, where he no longer reads from the Haggadah. I wander through the living room, where he no longer sits watching television or gazing out the window to see who's coming or going. I wander through the front hallway, where his motorized chair sits unplugged at the base of the stairs.

Toward the end of his life, when he had time to write, he didn't write about the Bonus March. Instead, he chose to focus on this time long before I was born, when he had witnessed the quiet kindness and efficiency of a respected professional in the field he had chosen. He wrote small stories about a doctor he admired, one who inspired him, one who was efficient, understated, and, above all, decent. And maybe when it came down to it, this was what was most important to my dad—small acts of kindness and decency in his own profession during a time when he was beginning to transform his life from that of the kid on the old West Side to the successful doctor he would become. The majesty of the title on my father's pages, "The Humanity of Man," doesn't quite match the small stories he wrote. He was probably thinking of "Dr. O" when he wrote "Humanity," but when I see that word, I think of my father.

V

Nora has finally gone to bed and I'm reading *A Writer's Diary*, by Virginia Woolf, on the couch when my mother enters the den with three sheets of notebook paper.

"Did I ever tell you your father began to write his autobiography?" she asks.

"You mean those pages upstairs?"

"No," she says. "He wrote this at the kitchen table. It's not much really. I can show you if you want."

"I'd like to see it."

"It's so sad," she says. "It's really a sad story."

I glance over the pages. The story my father tells is one I already know by now—born in Lying-In Hospital in 1925; a year under a doctor's care at the Illinois Research Hospital; Marshall High School; college; medical school; marriage; a house in West Rogers Park. There are only a few details I hadn't been aware of before—the address of a clinic where he worked, the names of medical residents he lived with, the fact that in his grammar school, students were assigned seats according to their purported intelligence, and my father sat in the first seat in the first row.

"What's sad about it?" I ask my mother.

"Read the last line."

I look down to the bottom of the page: "It's a beautiful day and I am in the kitchen continuing to write this sort of biography," my dad writes. During those last months, he spent a lot of time at that kitchen table. I would see him scribbling there, trying to sketch, staring into space, trying to sleep. "If things continue on as they are," my father concludes, "I will be content, if not actually happy."

"It's sad, isn't it?" my mother says. "It's beyond sad really."

But as I read, I'm not filled with sadness. Instead, I feel, if not happiness, at least some sense of balance. Through this journey, I've still been viewing the fact that my dad didn't write his book as some small tragedy, a sign that his life was incomplete, that he hadn't done all that he wanted. Maybe if he'd had other interests, I've still been thinking, maybe if he'd continued to pursue his art, maybe then . . .

Well, maybe then what? I wonder now.

I've never tried to finish that sentence, but now I think it might go something like this: Maybe he wouldn't have seemed so satisfied with a life in which I never felt as if I played all that great a part, with a history in which I often felt less like a pivotal and memorable moment than, well, like a bonus march. A book left unfinished, a dream left unfulfilled would have hinted at some dissatisfaction that on some level I might have wanted him to feel. But toward the end, he shows little sign of feeling dissatisfied; on paper, he presents the simple facts of his life, seems to see no need to adorn them with embellishments or exaggerations; he says he feels nearly content with where he has arrived.

All this time, I've been searching for reasons why my father barely ever left Chicago, even when he was healthy enough to do so, why he never wrote his book, when he seemed to have the energy and the time. And the answer might just be that he didn't need to, that he'd already arrived in a place where he belonged, doing something that he felt mattered. My dad's father spent his life searching, working, moving. For my dad, contentment might well have meant staying put. In the end, what need was there to go to Washington, D.C., to see what remained of the camps at Anacostia, why drive all the way out to the Hoover Library, which was way farther than Faye's, why go to Los Angeles or Hyde Park or Indianapolis, when he felt satisfied in Chicago? He'd just stay on Mozart Street in West Rogers Park—6:00 A.M. work, 2:00 P.M. home, a small but efficient life of service, and maybe that was just fine by him.

"That Rosebud you're trying to find out about— Maybe that was something he lost." The line from my mother's favorite movie returns to me. Maybe that Rosebud I've been looking for was something my father didn't need to find.

"Do you really think it's so sad?" I ask my mother.

"Don't you think it is?" she asks.

SIDNEY

In the Archives of Traditional Music at Indiana University, I wear a pair of headphones as I listen to reel-to-reel tapes. In the late 1950s, my dad bought a Bell reel-to-reel tape recorder, and every so often, he would gather the family around the microphone. He would tape birthday parties, my mom's brother Norm Herstein, his wife, Roz, and their daughters reading poetry and history, a radio quiz show on which my cousin Paulie Rosenberg competed. A 1964 tape features my mom, brother, and sister reading aloud letters my mom sent home to my dad when she and my siblings took a trip to visit national parks. On the tape, my father quizzes them, makes wiseass remarks, or tells my brother to stop monkeying around with the microphone.

This is the first time I've heard my father's voice in three years, and I am amazed to hear how vital he sounds, how young, how engaged. But there's very little content here that would interest anyone outside of my family. Nevertheless, I'm marching onward, persevering, listening to every tape. I want to make sure there's nothing I haven't tried, no explanation I've missed.

One of the tapes here is labeled "Bradley's 5th Birthday Party," and although my father usually wrote down the names of all the people who talked on his tapes, this one is marked "EVERYBODY." At first, it is difficult to identify individual voices or what they're saying. But I can hear old-world accents, voices that belong to people who died before I was born or before I was old enough to understand or appreciate their stories. I hear relatives and friends greet my brother, wish him happy birthday, kibbitz. In one conversation, I hear my grandfather's voice—I haven't heard Sam Langer since I was about five years old, and he never sounded this lively to me. Sam needles my dad about the fact that there aren't any mezuzahs in his house, and the dialogue sounds as if it comes right out of some nostalgic Neil Simon play:

SAM LANGER

He hasn't even got a yarmulke here, ya see?

(*Calling out*)

Ya remember a yarmulke? That's what we useta wear on Fourteenth Street. Ya know how many mezuzahs ya got here? Ya haven't even got 'em in here. And how come you took the mezuzahs off the door?

SEYMOUR LANGER
Who?

SAM LANGER
You.

SEYMOUR LANGER
I didn't take 'em off.

SAM LANGER
Somebody took 'em off. ,

SEYMOUR LANGER
I couldn't tell you.

SAM LANGER
Every door should have a mezuzah.

SEYMOUR LANGER
Who says so?

SAM LANGER
I say so.

SEYMOUR LANGER
What's it gonna help?

I keep listening. The recording stops for a while. Then it picks up
again. It's some time later in the birthday party. My grandfather is
now talking to another man about the old country he and his family
left behind.

"I'm forty years from over there away," Sam Langer says in his distinctly Yiddish cadence, "and our family there, not a one of them is living. Not a one is living. Nobody living from our family over there. I had a cousin. Over there. *Mein* cousin, he was a general, Sidney."

I begin to listen with greater attention, trying to figure out who is being discussed.

"A general in the Polish army," I hear Sam say, "in Lvov. Sidney, he was born in Lvov. His father had a big department store there. He kept the Russian army outta there. Starved them outta there. For three months. They couldn't get no deliveries. He comes up to the front. He says to the Russians, 'Okay, you can take the city now.' And they killed him. And they took the city. He was a general, *mein* cousin Sidney."

I stop the tape. I rewind. And I listen to it again.

And again.

Sidney. He was a general. Mein cousin Sidney.

Sidney. It is the name my father was born with, the name my father told his best friend, Lenny, that he didn't like, the name my father told me was changed to fool the dybbuk so that he would live. My grandfather seems to be telling a more detailed version of the same story my father used to allude to—a Polish general who fought the Russians in World War I. The story takes place in Lvov, the major city nearest to Rachin, in Galicia, where my grandfather lived before he journeyed to Ellis Island. My father never told me the whole story, and when he told it, he left out the name of the general.

I play the tape again and again to make sure I've heard correctly. I have. My grandfather is saying "Sidney."

To me, the word *Sidney* is as meaningful but also as elusive as any word inscribed on a child's sled burning in a fireplace.

I listen again. And again. And as I listen, a new story begins to form in my mind, one that goes like this:

A man from Rachin moves to America, where he works as a civilian contractor taking care of mules during World War One. He is the cousin of a military man who remains behind in Europe and dies after trying to save the city where he was born. In 1925, the man from Rachin and his wife have a son and decide to name him after the man who died. But the boy is born with a limp and nearly dies of pneumonia at the age of two. His name is changed from Sidney to Seymour, perhaps to fool the dybbuk, perhaps because the boy will never live up to the history of the man for whom he was named. The boy grows and sees his friends and his relatives go off to fight in a war, while he stays behind, physically unable to join them. He goes on to lead a rich and fulfilling life, and yet, for years, there is some sense of guilt, of not measuring up. When he tells stories of his life, he embellishes them, feels a need to exaggerate details. He grows interested in war stories, senses that the men who served during those wars didn't get the honor they deserved. Someday, he thinks, he will write a book about some of those men. But toward the end of his life, he finds contentment in the life he has led, realizes that his own life has value, and he no longer needs to write his book.

Of course this cannot be the whole story; of course if my father were alive, he would probably find the story too simplistic and sentimental, too much like the stories I write, not enough like the nonfiction he reads. *I don't know if it's true or it isn't,* I can hear him say. *I don't know if you're right or you're not.* Still, the story of a man who at first feels he doesn't quite measure up to his father's history, who wants to write a book to honor that history, then, in the process of looking back, realizes his own life has value resonates for me, and when my daughter is old enough to understand it, it will be one of the stories I will tell her.

2008

I'm back with Nora at my mother's house in West Rogers Park. I trust my memory, but I've been photographing every room in the house anyway just to make sure my memories have been accurate. I've photographed the basement and the first floor and the upstairs bedrooms. I've photographed my father's artwork—his sketches, his barium-barrel collages, his sculptures. I've taken pictures of the front yard and the backyard, of my mother's garden, of the unopened shirts in my father's drawers, of the pressed shirts in his closet. While Nora is napping, my mother is sitting on the floor of the den, reading the *Odyssey,* when she looks up from her book.

"Do me a favor," she says. "Don't take any pictures of me."

I put down the camera.

On my mother's desk in the den is a small album of family photographs. On the cover is a picture of my dad in his armchair at the kitchen table—smiling yet dubious, as always. I flip through the book, and I find a slip of lined yellow paper inside it. I see my father's handwriting. I take the paper and head out to the front stoop to read it. I watch the neighbors pass—kids on tricycles, men in dark suits, and women in long dresses heading to shul.

I remember telling stories here, listening to my father tell them. And I've been telling a story about the stories he didn't tell me, about the pieces he left out, about the stories his country left out, too, because they didn't fit in with some grand, heroic tale. And now, as my daughter sleeps in my mother's house, I'm thinking about the stories that I haven't told her yet, about the pieces I'll leave out of my stories. I'm wondering if I'll tell her about tragedies and failures, about arguments and sickness. I wonder if I'll tell her stories about mistakes I made, about moments when I was less than heroic or admirable. I wonder if I'll tell her about times when I messed up, about dreams I wanted to achieve but never did. Or if I'll just try to tell her the happy or funny parts, the inspiring stories, the way my father always did. I wonder if I'll just leave out the rest. I wonder how much I've already left out, how much I've already chosen not to tell.

Sitting on the stoop of my mother's house, I glance down at the few sentences my father wrote. The handwriting is shaky again; he must have written this late in his life.

"The moments, hours, days and years pass by and before you know it, yesterday's newborn kids are grown," he wrote. "Today's parents are tomorrow's grandparents. And so it goes. Main streams go on to be tributaries.

"Life on the planet earth," he wrote, "is amazing."

ACKNOWLEDGMENTS

This book has been written with the cooperation and support of many people, first and foremost my mother, Esther Langer; my daughter, Nora Langer Sissenich; my partner, Beate Sissenich; my editor, Cindy Spiegel; and my agent, Marly Rusoff, all of whom inspired me to write it. I would also like to thank the members of my father's Marshall High School Bull Session, many of whom contributed to the book. I must also thank various Langers (Bradley, Donna, Jerome, Jerry, Julie, Karen, Sylvie, et al.). And many, many thanks for all sorts of reasons to Joan Afton, Tom Allen, Dan Andries, James Atlas, Steve Barkin, Ira Bell and Claire Pensyl, Pepi Bernstein, Bobst Library of New York University, John Edward Bodnar, Erik Bucy, Norman and Bess Budow, Robert Clark, Cambria County Historical Society, Cambria County Library, Ted Carmines, Chicago History Museum, Andrew Chou, Lida Churchville, Paul B. Creamer, Ray DesRosiers, Stuart Dybek, Lucy Eisenberg, Dan Epstein, Rachel Fedewa, Franklin D. Roosevelt Presidential Library and Museum, Henry Louis Gates, Jr., Jennifer

Gilmore, Mark Gleason, Martin Gorbien, Marilyn Graff at the Indiana University Archives of Traditional Music, Julie Grau, Patricia Hampl, Mary Herczog, Evelyn Brooks Higginbotham, Historical Society of Washington, D.C., Herbert Hoover Presidential Library and Museum, Joseph Horowitz, Joseph Hovish of the American Legion, Spencer Howard, staff of the Indonesian embassy, Jeff Isaac, Sarah Kerr, Senator John F. Kerry, Gretchen Koss, Alex Kotlowitz, Jerome Kramer, Hana Landes, Seymour and Marlene Levine, Lester Lewis, Ross McElwee, Colleen McKnight, Millicent Marks, Kate Steffes Mattson, Elena Melendez, Susan O'Donovan, Norman Podhoretz, Leonard and Sue Primer, Alison Rich, Stephen and Adrianne Roderick, Robin Rummel, Mihai Radelescu, Wendy Salinger, Mitchell Schorow, Stephanie Schorow, Naaman Seigle, Sheldon Schoneberg, Gene Shalit, Jerry and Pepi Singer, Dr. Dmitros Spigos, Bella Stein, Seymour Sudar, U.S. Library of Congress, David Wade and Julie Wirkkala at the office of Senator John Kerry, Chip Wadsworth, Timothy Walch, Meghan Walker, Irv Warso and Beverly Sokol, Howard Watt, Andy Wilbur, and Teresa Zamarron.

NOTES

27 the occasional coauthored medical paper: J. Robert Thompson and Seymour Langer, "Eosinophilic Granuloma of the Lungs: Roentgenologic
and Pathologic Features," *Chest* 46, no. 5 (1964): 553–561.

27 letters to the *American Journal:* Seymour S. Langer, "Square Chest Films
Revisited: Experience with 16 x 16 Inch Siemens Chest Films," *American Journal of Roentgenology* 129 (1982): 1242.

38 Martin Luther King, Jr., who credited: "U.S. 'Plays Roulette with Riots,' "
Washington Post, April 7, 1968.

38 When he was advising President Nixon: Andrew Hunt, *The Turning,* 107.

38 but also Gen. George S. Patton: "Cavalry Major Evicts Veteran Who Saved
His Life in Battle," *New York Times,* July 30, 1932.

38 Maj. Dwight D. Eisenhower, who served: "MacArthur Held Fascination
for Ike," *Washington Post,* April 20, 1967.

38 Oregon laborer and veteran: Paul Dickson and Thomas B. Allen, *The Bonus
Army: An American Epic,* 56–57.

38 fascist party called the Khaki Shirts: "Waters to Form Fascist Group of
'Khaki Shirts,' " *Chicago Daily Tribune,* July 30, 1932.

38 Brig. Gen. Pelham D. Glassford: "Brig. Gen. P. D. Glassford Dead; Led
Police Against Bonus March," *New York Times,* August 10, 1959.

38 served as their treasurer: "B.E.F. Faces Hunger as Funds Give Out; Bakers' Aid Sought," *New York Times*, June 28, 1932.

38 Royal Robertson, an unemployed Hollywood actor: Dickson and Allen, *The Bonus Army*, 145.

39 William Randolph Hearst: Ibid., 284.

39 ire of the notorious Hays Commission: "Gabriel Film Sent Back to Hollywood," *New York Times*, March 17, 1933.

40 unfairly characterizing their march: Dickson and Allen, *The Bonus Army*, 197.

40 "The veterans had been denied": Bradley Langer, "The Bonus March," 10.

40 another bonus march: Eleanor Roosevelt, *The Autobiography of Eleanor Roosevelt*, 175.

40 FDR enticed some of the campers: "Roosevelt Blocks Paying Cash Bonus; Aids Idle Veterans," *New York Times*, May 12, 1933.

40 hundreds who took those jobs: "Hopkins Denies Error by FERA Cost Gale Toll," *Washington Post*, September 6, 1935.

40 bonus bill in 1935: Dickson and Allen, *The Bonus Army*, 230.

40 the acts of the marchers: Ibid., 266–277.

46 Farther up Pennsylvania Avenue: "All Bonus Camps Burned by Troops After Riot," *Los Angeles Times*, July 29, 1932.

46 Surround the affected area: Ibid.

46 "Let's get him": Ibid.

46 "For God's sake": Pelham D. Glassford, testimony before the grand jurors for the July 1932 term, August 1, 1932.

47 Bonus Army member William Hushka: "Battle of Washington," *Time*, August 8, 1932.

47 another marcher, Eric Carlson: "Bayonets Propel B.E.F. Campers from Washington," *B.E.F. News*, August 6, 1932.

47 A third veteran, John Hall: "Casualty List Issued in Bonus Army Riots," *Los Angeles Times*, July 29, 1932.

47 "It was a bad-looking mob": "Fear Cited of Revolt," *Los Angeles Times*, July 29, 1932.

48 Evalyn Walsh McLean, a fixture: Evalyn Walsh McLean, with Boyden Sparkes, *Father Struck It Rich*, 303.

52 ARMY NURSE SUFFERS: "Army Nurse Suffers Breakdown at Camp," *B.E.F. News*, July 16, 1932.

52 "Destitute Mother Searches": "Destitute Mother Searches for Lost Son," *B.E.F. News*, July 9, 1932.

52 "Need of Milk": "Need of Milk for Babies of B.E.F. Stirs Veterans," *B.E.F. News*, July 30, 1932.

53 They played at Griffith Stadium: "Bonus Groups Ignore Police Plea to Leave," *Washington Post,* June 9, 1932.

63 In Cook County: "Foreclosures Hit All Time High in December," *Chicago Daily Tribune,* January 13, 1932.

63 At Chicago's Majestic Theatre: Eve Cousin, "Chicago Society Backs Benefit Stage Show for and by Jobless," *Chicago Daily Tribune,* April 17, 1932.

63 On Twenty-third and Michigan: Rev. John Evans, "Church's Bread Line to End for Lack of Funds," *Chicago Daily Tribune,* April 22, 1932.

63 And at the railyards: "Capital Police Uneasy Over Bonus Army," *Chicago Daily Tribune,* May 27, 1932.

63 Bonus veterans raised money: "Bonus Brigade Finds Chicago a Chill Host," *Chicago Daily Tribune,* June 5, 1932.

63 The only articles I've tracked down: "Nominate Star West Side Seniors," *Chicago Daily Tribune,* January 3, 1943.

64 Another *Tribune* article: "1,700 Seniors Graduated from 10 West Side High Schools," *Chicago Daily Tribune,* January 31, 1943.

64 a one-act play: David Mamet, *The Old Neighborhood,* 17.

66 P.O.W., as it turns out: Hyman L. Meutes, ed., *History of the Jews in Chicago,* 670.

83 veterans may have been selling apples: Virginia Gardener, " 'Now We Can Eat!' Exclaim Shabby Vets in Bonus Line," *Chicago Daily Tribune,* March 3, 1931.

97 But Pashkow invented Kayo in 1929: Kenan Heise, "Aaron Pashkow, 90, of Chocolate Products," *Chicago Tribune,* April 17, 1986.

102 "For God's sake, take this gasoline": F. Raymond Daniell, "B.E.F. Last-Enders Cling to Their Camp," *New York Times,* August 6, 1932.

102 slept near the merry-go-round: "Troops Guard Johnstown as Bonus Army Digs In," *Los Angeles Times,* July 31, 1932.

109 in such locations as Waterbury, Maryland: "Ritchie Assails Camp Project," *Los Angeles Times,* August 2, 1932.

109 the president of Mexico: "Mexico Bars Colony," *Chicago Daily Tribune,* August 12, 1932.

109 In Chicago: "Bonus Hikers Bivouac Here on Sidewalk," *Chicago Daily Tribune,* August 5, 1932.

109 in City Hall Park: "500 of Bonus Army Arrive in the City," *New York Times,* August 8, 1932.

109 on Greene Street: "Rally to Protest Veterans' Eviction," *New York Times,* August 1, 1932.

109 attempted to camp: "Shacktown Pulls Through the Winter," *New York Times,* March 26, 1933.

109 In *To Have and Have Not:* Ernest Hemingway, *To Have and Have Not,* 207.

109 In 1933: "Bonus March Dramatized," *New York Times,* October 23, 1933.

110 "I'm just a poor boy": *The Bonus Army,* music and lyrics by Al Carmines, book by David Epstein, unpublished manuscript, Judson Memorial Church Archive, Bobst Library, New York University.

110 "The piece covers predictable ground": Gerald Rabkin, *Soho Weekly,* March 4, 1976.

110 "there's never any doubt": Cynthia Lee Jenner, "Twice the Trouble," *The Villager,* March 4, 1976.

111 (such as having Eleanor): "First Lady Trods Mud," *Los Angeles Times,* May 17, 1933.

112 Socialist candidate Norman Thomas: "Thomas Denounces Tactics of Hoover," *New York Times,* July 31, 1932.

112 My dad worked: Edward Schreiber, "City's Top 50 Employees Fare Well," *Chicago Tribune,* November 21, 1965.

116 "In a figurative sense": Statement on veterans affairs, at www.specter.senate.gov.

117 Kerry's grandfather was born Jewish: Douglas Brinkley, *Tour of Duty: John Kerry and the Vietnam War.*

117 "In the sad aftermath": H. L. Mencken, "H. L. Mencken Gives the Boys a Hand by Supporting Bonus Stand," *B.E.F. News,* July 23, 1932.

125 "Yours is the only daily newspaper": Norm Budow, *Chicago Daily Tribune,* May 3, 1954.

127 he sang Pete Seeger's: *Veterans for Peace Newsletter,* Summer 2004, 11.

145 collapsing twice on account of the heat: "Marines Called, Leave Capitol; March Goes On," *Washington Post,* July 15, 1932.

145 Three years later: "Roy Robertson Is Here Again," *Washington Post,* January 27, 1935.

145 Less than three years after that: "Bonus Army Leader Dies," *Los Angeles Times,* January 10, 1938.

145 died in 1959 in Laguna Beach: "Brig. Gen. P. D. Glassford Dead; Led Police Against Bonus March" *New York Times,* August 10, 1959.

145 working as an inspector: "Ex-Bonus Army Leader Has Job on Bay Bridge," *Los Angeles Times,* October 15, 1933.

148 "Father, mother, five children": J. Prentice Murphy, "Report on Bonus Force Emergency Camp, Johnstown, Penna, Also Other Kindred Matters and Visits," August 10, 1932.

161 holing up in the Salvation Army: "War Veterans Spur Plea to Leave Capital," *Chicago Tribune,* June 5, 1932.

161 in such towns as Roby: "500 on Way from Chicago," *Chicago Daily Tribune,* June 1, 1932.

161 and Seymour, Indiana: "Bonus Army Moves Slowly over Indiana," *New York Times,* May 27, 1932.

163 Before the march: Dickson and Allen, *The Bonus Army,* 48–49.

163 at the 1932 national convention: "Summary of Proceedings," Fourteenth Annual National Convention of the American Legion, Portland, Oregon, September 12–15.

191 "I think this is the first": "Interview with General MacArthur by the Press at 11:00 PM," released by the U.S. War Department, July 29, 1932.

194 "Everyone exclaims that he is not": Letter from Lou Henry Hoover to Allan Hoover, undated; Allan Hoover Papers—correspondence with Lou Henry Hoover—May–June 1932; Herbert Hoover Presidential Library, West Branch, Iowa.

195 "white man by the name of Lang": Confidential report on meeting of the Workers Ex-Serviceman's League, July 2, 1932, signed by J. Apostolides and A. E. Fredette.

207 In January 1936, the bonus bill: Dickson and Allen, *The Bonus Army,* 253–254.

207 checks started going out: "2,670,000 Bonus Letters in Mail for Vets Today," *Chicago Daily Tribune,* June 15, 1936.

218 There's a picture: Untitled article by Dr. Seymour Sidney Langer, *Physicians Weekly,* September 23, 1985.

BIBLIOGRAPHY

Anderson, Sherwood. *Memoirs*. New York: Harcourt, Brace, 1942.

Barber, Lucy G. *Marching on Washington*. Berkeley: University of California Press, 2002.

Best, Gary Dean. *FDR and the Bonus Marchers, 1933–1935*. Westport, Connecticut: Praeger, 1992.

Brandt, E. N. *Growth Company: Dow Chemical's First Century*. East Lansing: Michigan State University Press, 1997.

Brinkley, Douglas. *Tour of Duty: John Kerry and the Vietnam War*. New York: William Morrow, 2004.

Cowley, Malcolm. *The Dream of the Golden Mountains: Remembering the 1930s*. New York: Viking, 1980.

Cronin, A. J. *The Citadel*. Toronto: Ryerson Press, 1945.

De Kruif, Paul. *Microbe Hunters*. New York: Pocket Books, 1959.

Dickson, Paul, and Thomas B. Allen. *The Bonus Army: An American Epic*. New York: Walker & Company, 2004.

Dos Passos, John. *In All Countries*. New York: Harcourt, Brace, 1934.

Eisenhower, Dwight D. *Eisenhower: The Prewar Diaries and Selected Papers, 1905–1941*. Baltimore: Johns Hopkins University Press, 1988.

———. *At Ease: Stories I Tell to Friends*. Garden City, New York: Doubleday, 1967.

Hemingway, Ernest. *To Have and Have Not.* New York: Charles Scribner's Sons, 1937.

———. "Who Murdered the Vets?" *New Masses,* September 17, 1935.

Hoover, Herbert. *The Great Depression, 1929–1941.* Vol. 3 of *The Memoirs of Herbert Hoover.* New York: Macmillan, 1951.

Hunt, Andrew. *The Turning: A History of Vietnam Veterans Against the War.* New York: NYU Press, 2001.

Langer, Bradley. "The Bonus March." Unpublished research paper written for U.S. History class in Mather High School, circa 1970–1971.

Lee, Norman D. "A History of Bio-Science Laboratories." *Clinical Chemistry,* 40, no. 1 (1994): 149–157.

Lisio, Donald J. *The President and Protest: Hoover, MacArthur, and the Bonus Riot.* New York: Fordham University Press, 1994.

Mamet, David. *The Old Neighborhood.* New York: Samuel French, Inc., 1998.

Manchester, William. *The Glory and the Dream.* Boston: Little, Brown, 1974.

Mankiewicz, Herman J., and Orson Welles. "The shooting script." *The Citizen Kane Book.* New York: Limelight Editions, 1984.

McLean, Evalyn Walsh, with Boyden Sparkes. *Father Struck It Rich.* Boston: Little, Brown, 1936.

Meisel, Henry. *The Second Bonus Army.* Clintonville, Wisconsin: n.p., 1933.

Meites, Hyman L., ed. *History of the Jews in Chicago.* Chicago: Chicago Jewish Historical Society and Wellington Publishing, 1990.

Podhoretz, Norman. *Breaking Ranks: A Political Memoir.* New York: Harper & Row, 1979.

Rogers, Will. "Will Rogers Remarks." *Los Angeles Times,* July 29, 1932.

Roosevelt, Eleanor. *The Autobiography of Eleanor Roosevelt.* 1937. Reprint, New York: Da Capo, 1992.

Specter, Arlen, with Frank J. Scaturro. *Never Give In: Battling Cancer in the Senate.* New York: Macmillan, 2008.

Stevenson, William. *A Man Called Intrepid: The Secret War.* New York: Macmillan, 1976.

Terkel, Studs. *Hard Times: An Oral History of the Great Depression.* New York: Pantheon Books, 1970.

Thompson, J. Robert, and Seymour Langer. "Eosinophilic Granuloma of the Lungs: Roentgenologic and Pathologic Features." *Chest* 46, no. 5 (1964): 553–561.

Thorek, Max. *A Surgeon's World: An Autobiography.* New York: J. B. Lippincott, 1943.

Tuchman, Barbara. *Practicing History: Selected Essays.* New York: Alfred A. Knopf, 1981.

Van Rijn, Guido. *Roosevelt's Blues: African-American Blues and Gospel Songs on FDR.* Jackson: University of Mississippi Press, 1997.

Vidal, Gore. *Screening History.* Cambridge: Harvard University Press, 1992.

Waters, W. W., and William C. White. *B.E.F.: The Whole Story of the Bonus Army.* New York: John Day Company, 1933.

Weaver, John D. *Another Such Victory.* New York: Viking Press, 1948.

———. "Bonus March." *American Heritage,* June 1963.

Webb, Robert N. *The Bonus March on Washington, D.C., May–June, 1932.* New York: Franklin Watts, 1969.

Wolf, Naomi. *Give Me Liberty: A Handbook for American Revolutionaries.* New York: Simon & Schuster, 2008.

Wolff, William Almon. *Murder at Endor.* New York: Minton, Balch, & Company, 1933.

MOST FREQUENTLY CONSULTED NEWSPAPERS

B.E.F. News, Chicago Tribune, Johnstown *Tribune-Democrat, Los Angeles Times, New York Times, Washington Post.*

FILMS

Gabriel Over the White House (dir. Gregory La Cava, 1933); *Gold Diggers of 1933* (dir. Mervyn LeRoy, 1933); *The March of the Bonus Army* (dir. Robert Uth, 2006); *Sherman's March* (dir. Ross McElwee, 1986); *Washington Merry-Go-Round* (dir. James Cruze, 1932).

ABOUT THE TYPE

This book was set in Caslon, a typeface first designed in 1722 by William Caslon. Its widespread use by most English printers in the early eighteenth century soon supplanted the Dutch typefaces that had formerly prevailed. The roman is considered a "workhorse" typeface due to its pleasant, open appearance, while the italic is exceedingly decorative.